Richard Dembo
James Schmeidler

Family Empowerment Intervention
An Innovative Service for High-Risk Youths and Their Families

Pre-publication
REVIEWS,
COMMENTARIES,
EVALUATIONS . . .

"*Family Empowerment Intervention* is unique in that it provides a nice opportunity for practitioners to assess the feasibility and value of the FEI approach. This is accomplished through a very readable examination of the theory and rationale behind the use of FEI interventions and a description of clinical goals, the curricula sequence and content, phases of treatment, staff training requirements, and specific strategies for implementing the approach in practice settings. The book also describes a range of family dynamics and issues addressed by FEI. It is rare to see the level of detail describing implementation procedures for operationalizing the clinical approach. For example, a comprehensive set of structured clinical exercises and activities is provided that can be used to engage families in FEI treatment. This book should serve as a valuable resource for those interested in developing innovative strategies for high-risk youths and their families."

Roger H. Peters, PhD
Professor, Department
of Mental Health Law and Policy,
University of South Florida,
Louis de Parte Florida
Mental Health Institute, Tampa

More pre-publication
REVIEWS, COMMENTARIES, EVALUATIONS . . .

"Dembo and Schmeidler add to the growing arsenal of effective treatment interventions with *Family Empowerment Intervention*. In this book they provide a comprehensive overview of FEI, a systems-oriented, low-cost intervention delivered in the home by trained nontherapists for high-risk youths who have been arrested and their families. They also present findings from their long-term outcome studies of the impact of the FEI on a group of over 300 arrested youths processed at a Florida juvenile assessment center. These data supplement their earlier reports on their short-term outcomes of the intervention. The study is well designed, comprehensive in scope, successfully conducted, and carefully analyzed. While results are somewhat mixed depending on the particular outcome variable examined (e.g., delinquent behavior, drug use, emotional/psychological functioning), the long-term data continue to support the main hypothesis of the study—that empowering parents through FEI would improve client youths' behavior and functioning and reduce recidivism. In addition, the authors document the cost savings to the justice system from implementing the intervention. Their data highlights the promise of this low-cost in-home intervention. More research on FEI is clearly necessary. Nonetheless, this work represents an important contribution to the field."

Joseph J. Cocozza, PhD
Vice President for Research,
Director of National GAINS Center,
Policy Research Associates,
Delmar, NY

The Haworth Press®
New York • London • Oxford

Family Empowerment Intervention

An Innovative Service for High-Risk Youths and Their Families

HAWORTH Criminal Justice,
Forensic Behavioral Sciences,
& Offender Rehabilitation
Nathaniel J. Pallone, PhD
Senior Editor

Family Empowerment Intervention

An Innovative Service for High-Risk Youths and Their Families

Richard Dembo
James Schmeidler

The Haworth Press®
New York • London • Oxford

The Haworth Press, Inc., 10 Alice Street, Binghamton, NY 13904-1580.

Cover design by Marylouise E. Doyle.

Library of Congress Cataloging-in-Publication Data

Dembo, Richard.
    Family empowerment intervention : an innovative service for high-risk youths and their families / Richard Dembo, James Schmeidler.
        p. cm.
    Includes bibliographical references and index.
    ISBN 0-7890-1572-2 (alk. paper) — ISBN 0-7890-1573-0 (alk. paper)
    1. Social work with youth. 2. Youth—Family relationships. 3. Family social work. 4. Youth—Services for. 5. Family. I. Schmeidler, James. II. Title.

HV1421 .D45 2002
362.7'083—dc21
                                                                                                    2001051857

CONTENTS

ABOUT THE AUTHORS

Richard Dembo, PhD, is Professor of Criminology at the University of South Florida in Tampa. He has conducted extensive research on the relationship between drug use and delinquency. Dr. Dembo has published two books, co-authored a monograph, and has written over 150 articles, book chapters, and reports in the fields of criminology, substance abuse, mental health, and program evaluation. He is a member of the editorial boards of *The International Journal of the Addictions* (recently renamed *Substance Use and Misuse*); *Violence, Aggression, and Terrorism;* the *Journal of Drug Issues;* and the *Journal of Child and Adolescent Substance Abuse.*

Dr. Dembo has served as consultant to the National Institute on Drug Abuse, the National Institute of Mental Health, the Center for Substance Abuse Treatment, the National Institute of Justice, and the National Science Foundation. He is a former Chair of the American Sociological Association Section on Alcohol and Drugs. Dr. Dembo helped develop the Hillsborough County Juvenile Assessment Center in Tampa, Florida, and supports JAC operations by completing special research studies and by developing, implementing, and evaluating the impact of innovative service delivery projects for youths processed at the JAC and their families.

James Schmeidler, PhD, is Assistant Clinical Professor in the Departments of Psychiatry and Biomathematical Sciences at the Mt. Sinai Medical School in New York City. He has also worked for the New York State Office of Alcoholism and Substance Abuse Services since 1973. Drs. Dembo and Schmeidler met in 1973, when they were both employed by the state agency then known as the New York State Drug Abuse Control Commission. They worked together on a number of projects for the state agency and continued collaborating after Dr. Dembo left the DACC in 1976. Over 80 published papers and book chapters have resulted from their collaborative efforts. In addition to assisting researchers on research design, instrument construction, and data analysis issues, Dr. Schmeidler pursues statistical research on multiple comparisons.

Foreword

Although the journey has been slow, the field is beginning to learn that some things do work. Despite declining rates of adolescent violent crime, we continue our "get tough" attitude and policies toward youths who become involved with the juvenile justice system. The past decade has seen more youths transferred to criminal court, longer sentences for youthful offenders, and lower minimum ages at which juveniles can be prosecuted as adults. Our persistent attitudes reflect the confluence of a number of factors, including remnants of the significant rise in violent crimes that occurred in the late 1980s and early 1990s; publicity surrounding visible and frightening cases of violent acts by youths across the country; and the firmly held belief that we may as well put them behind bars since nothing else works— no treatments or interventions have been found that result in positive and long-term improvements. If we cannot cure them, we can at least keep them off the streets.

Fortunately, over the past few years a number of new community-based approaches and treatments have been developed that have been able to demonstrate successful outcomes for high-risk and delinquent youths. Some of these, such as multisystemic therapy, have been systematically researched on a number of groups of youths across the country using carefully designed clinical trials, and have consistently shown positive outcomes on a number of dimensions including recidivism, psychiatric symptomology, and drug use. Other approaches such as functional family therapy and multidimensional treatment foster care have also shown impressive results with youths involved in delinquent behavior, alcohol, or other drug abuse.

These evidence-based interventions have begun to receive attention and, in many communities, are being adopted in an effort to both effectively address the multiple and interrelated problems of these youths and their families and to generate an alternative to the cycle of arrest, incarceration, release, and recidivism.

Dembo and Schmeidler add to the growing arsenal of effective treatment interventions with this book. Their work provides a comprehensive overview of the Family Empowerment Intervention (FEI), a systems-oriented, low-cost intervention delivered in the home by trained nontherapists for high-risk youths who have been arrested and their families. They describe the theoretical foundation of the intervention and detail the goals, strategies, and intervention phases used in FEI. Much of the remainder of the book is devoted to presenting the results of their short-term (twelve months) and long-term (up to forty-eight months) outcome studies of the impact of the FEI on a group of over 300 arrested youths processed at a Florida juvenile assessment center. The study is well designed (youths and their families were randomly assigned to either FEI or a comparison intervention), comprehensive in scope (examining fourteen different outcome variables focused on delinquent behavior, drug use, and emotional/psychological functioning), successfully conducted (with retention rates for the three waves of follow-up interviews ranging from 76 to 86 percent) and carefully analyzed. Although results are somewhat mixed depending on the particular outcome variable examined and the length of follow-up, the data support the main hypothesis of the study—that empowering parents through FEI would improve client youth's behavior and functioning and reduce recidivism. In addition, they are also able to demonstrate substantial cost savings to the justice system from implementing this intervention. Their analysis indicates savings of $4.7 million in cumulative direct costs over a three-year period.

Dembo and Schmeidler correctly conclude that their work highlights the promise of this intervention. More research on FEI and improvements to the intervention, several of which are suggested by the authors, are clearly necessary. Nonetheless, their work represents an important contribution to the field. While we are beginning to demonstrate that some things do work, we are also realizing how much more we need to learn about what works best for which population under which circumstances. Their work demonstrates that as an alternative to other approaches, FEI, a low-cost in-home intervention provided by trained nontherapists, deserves further exploration and investigation.

Depending on a number of factors—the nature of the family, the client's willingness and ability to be engaged, the range and severity of issues experienced by the youths, and available resources—different interventions may be more or less appropriate and effective. What this study shows is that in our attempts to address the problems of troubled youths and their families and reduce the flow of these youths deeper into the juvenile and eventually the adult criminal justice system, FEI must be considered along with the other developing strategies that are demonstrating that some things do work.

Joseph J. Cocozza, PhD
Policy Research Associates

Acknowledgments

The Youth Support Project was a demanding, growth-filled experience for us. Quality intervention services were needed. Over 850 in-depth interviews were completed with the youths involved in the various analyses. Tracking and completing follow-up interviews with them and their families often involved creativity and persistence. This project could not have been completed without the support of caring, dedicated staff.

All clinical, intervention, and project research staff are to be deeply thanked for their many contributions to the success of this project. Project Field Consultants are particularly deserving of appreciation. The Agency for Community Treatment Services, Inc. was a consistent supporter of our work, as was the Hillsborough County Sheriff's Office, the Hillsborough County School Board, the Florida Department of Juvenile Justice, and the Florida Department of Corrections. National Institute on Drug Abuse staff, particularly Dr. Peter Delany and Dr. Jerry Flanzer, deserve special thanks for their support. They provided continuous wisdom and assistance. We wish also to thank the many youths and families we served for their trust and the privilege of working with them.

Ms. Marianne Bell deserves special thanks for word processing numerous drafts of the book manuscript. She was always willing to help. Mr. Stephen Livingston provided a great service to this book by helping organize material at an early point from which this manuscript developed; and he provided valuable suggestions on the organization of the book.

Ms. Jean Shirhall, our editorial assistant, was a great resource to us. Her sharp editing and skill with words helped make various drafts of the book much more readable. We are deeply indebted to her.

We deeply appreciate Dr. Nathaniel J. Pallone's encouragement and support during the entire process. We have sought to do justice to his vision for this project.

Finally, we should like to publicly express heartfelt appreciation to our wives, Enid and Lucy. Their patience with long hours, and often weekends, of work was essential to the completion of the project. This book could never have been finished without their wisdom, advice, and support.

Preparation of this manuscript was supported by Grant # 1-R01-DA08707, funded by the National Institute on Drug Abuse. We are grateful for their support. However, the research results reported and the views expressed in this book do not necessarily imply any policy or research endorsement by the funding agency.

Chapter 1

The Need for Effective, Cost-Efficient Intervention Services for High-Risk Youths

Developing and implementing effective and cost-efficient intervention services for youths who use alcohol or other drugs and have related problems, including contact with the juvenile justice system, remain critical needs (Sherman et al., 1997). There are several reasons for this urgency.

First, there has been an increase in overall youth crime and its effects, as well as a growing awareness of the magnitude of these problems among various high-risk groups (Butts and Harrell, 1998). Although there are recent indications that violent crime among juveniles has decreased, youth crime overall remains at unacceptably high levels. For example, a study in Maricopa County (Phoenix, Arizona) involving 150,000 youths who reached age eighteen between 1980 and 1995, found that 46 percent of the males referred to juvenile court intake for the first time, and 27 percent of the females, were referred at least one more time. Nineteen percent of the males were eventually referred four or more times (Snyder and Sickmund, 1999). The juvenile population is expected to increase substantially in the next twenty years, which in turn threatens to increase further the burden on the juvenile justice system. National drug test studies (National Institute of Justice, 1999) of arrested juveniles continue to indicate high levels of drug use. This situation, together with the high rate of law-violation referrals to juvenile court (a 57 percent increase between 1980 and 1995), has resulted in increasingly backlogged juvenile court systems in many jurisdictions throughout the United States, less time for case deliberation and supervision, and less-effective placement in needed services (Snyder and Sickmund, 1995).

Second, service providers are challenged to address the multiple problems that are presented by youths in the juvenile justice system. Younger juveniles are being arrested more frequently, and they have many serious, interrelated problems, including drug use, educational deficits, emotional issues, and abuse and neglect histories (Dembo, Schmeidler, et al., 1998). Research has consistently documented that many juveniles entering the juvenile justice system have multiple personal, educational, and family problems (Dembo et al., 1996, 1989). The following problems are consistently reported by researchers:

- physical abuse (Dembo, Williams, and Schmeidler, 1998);
- sexual victimization (Dembo, Williams, and Schmeidler, 1998; Dembo, Wothke, Shemwell, et al., 2000);
- poor emotional/psychological functioning (Teplin and Swartz, 1989; Dembo, Williams, Berry, Getreu, et al., 1990; Timmons-Mitchell et al., 1999; Cocozza, 1997; Faenza and Siegfried, 1998), in particular, co-occurring mental health and drug abuse problems (Winters, 1998);
- poor educational functioning (Dembo, Williams, Schmeidler, and Howitt, 1991; Office of Juvenile Justice and Delinquency Prevention, 2000); and
- alcohol and other drug use (Dembo, Pacheco, Schmeidler, Fisher, et al., 1997a).

Many of these difficulties can be traced to family alcohol/other drug use, mental health problems, or criminal behavior these juveniles experienced when they were young (Dembo, Williams, Wotke, Schmeidler, et al., 1992; Dembo, Wotke, Seeberger, et al., 2000). *The interrelatedness of these problems urges that holistic, not sequential, services be developed for these juveniles and their families.* Unfortunately, juvenile justice agencies in most jurisdictions have limited resources for providing services, and many juveniles entering the juvenile justice system come from families lacking resources to pay for their care.

Third, minority (particularly African American and Hispanic) inner-city juveniles and their families continue to be underserved in regard to their mental health and substance-abuse service needs (Tolan, Ryan, and Jaffe, 1988; Sirles, 1990; Arcia et al., 1993; Dembo and Seeberger, 1999). These families tend to utilize substance abuse and mental health treatment services at lower rates (program entry, engagement, and duration) than do Caucasian families. Among the factors responsible for these differences are the generally lower income of black and Hispanic families (which leads to a reliance on inadequately funded public services), transportation problems, cultural insensitivity among service providers, and language differences (Espada, 1979; Arcia et al., 1993). In the absence of accessible intervention services, all too many minority youths entering the juvenile justice system will eventually become involved with the adult justice system and consume a large and growing amount of local, state, and national criminal justice and mental health resources as they grow older (Office of National Drug Control Policy, 1997). Further, minority, inner-city juveniles are often socialized in communities and families that are economically and socially stressed. The psychosocial strain experienced by these youths, including their witnessing violence and its effects (Crimmins et al., 2000), increases their risk of future drug use and delinquency/crime (Nurco, Balter, and Kinlock, 1994) and impedes their development as socially responsible and productive adults (LeBlanc, 1990).

Fourth, getting juveniles with substance abuse and/or related problems into treatment and keeping them there present considerable challenges (Battjes, Onken, and Delany, 1999). Many referred juveniles do not enter drug treatment, or leave prematurely, and this is associated with high rates of subsequent drug use, crime, and health and social problems. In addition, posttreatment relapse rates among adolescents with drug abuse problems (Catalano et al., 1990-1991), particularly those involved in the justice system, remain high (Armstrong and Altschuler, 1998), reflecting the often chronic nature of these problems. Insufficient numbers of staff working with delinquent juveniles and their families are trained to provide in-home intervention services (to increase family participation) and, where indicated, to link family members with other community resources. Such programs hold promise of improving services available to high-risk juveniles and their families, especially underserved African-American and Hispanic families (Alexander and Parsons, 1982).

Fifth, early intervention services are lacking at the front-end of the juvenile justice system (McBride et al., 1999). Such programs can involve youths and their families in needed services as soon after arrest as possible, while they are open to accessing help, and thereby reduce treatment entry and retention problems. Early intervention can cost effectively reduce the probability that troubled juveniles will continue criminal and high-risk health behavior into adulthood (Klitzner et al., 1991).

A major issue in research on intervention services for juveniles is that there is so little of it. Few programs divert resources from treatment to evaluate outcomes, especially long-term follow-up. Thus, it is often impossible to distinguish service or client characteristics associated with good outcomes. Rigorous, comprehensive studies of the impact and cost of juvenile interventions are rare (Dembo, Livingston, and Schmeidler, 2002). Overall, meta-analyses completed by Weisz et al. (1995) and Lipsey and Wilson (1998) have found a number of positive effects of treatment (e.g., reduced drug use and delinquency). Treatment for drug dependence and related psychosocial difficulties among adolescents has been found to be effective in reducing criminality (Anglin and Speckart, 1988). Programs based on social learning theories have been found to be particularly effective among adolescent drug abusers needing residential care (Jainchill et al., 2000). Treatment evaluation studies among adults show clear evidence regarding the efficacy and cost-effectiveness of treatment (Hubbard et al., 1989; Pickens, Leukefeld, and Schuster, 1991; Simpson, Wexler, and Inciardi, 1999). However, more evaluations of interventions involving adolescents are needed.

STRENGTHS AND LIMITATIONS OF CASE MANAGEMENT AND REFERRAL SERVICES

Case management and referral services are frequently used in the juvenile justice system (Ashery, 1992). They have proven valuable in a variety of settings. For example, Treatment Accountability for Safer Communities (TASC) programs attempt to provide linkages between the justice system and treatment agencies (McBride et al., 1999); many of these programs exist throughout the United States. The TASC model is a proven, well-defined intervention for substance-involved persons (Cook, 1992). In the most significant evaluation of TASC to date, Anglin et al. (1996) completed a quasi-experimental study of TASC programs in seven sites serving different client populations and operating in different environments; one of these sites (Orlando, Florida) had a juvenile TASC program. Each site involved a TASC group and a comparison group of persons placed on probation and receiving associated services. Overall, the evaluation found consistently favorable outcomes for TASC services across the sites (Anglin et al., 1996). Among other things, TASC clients were significantly more likely to obtain needed services than those in the comparison group.

The evaluation at the Orlando site focused on alcohol/other drug use, crime, and HIV-risk behaviors. Outcome analyses indicated that, compared to the non-TASC youths, juvenile TASC participants more often obtained needed services and reduced their sexual risk behaviors. The reduced sexual risk behaviors involved the increased use of condoms and a reduction in having sex while using drugs. However, no significant differences between the TASC and comparison groups were found in regard to alcohol/other drug use or criminal behavior over time (Anglin et al., 1996; McBride et al., 1999).

While Anglin and his colleagues (Anglin et al., 1996) found overall positive effects of the juvenile TASC program, they also noted the challenges to the effective delivery of TASC services. Among these were difficulties in providing comprehensive case management services, limitations in community treatment resources, and a weak or nonexistent coordinated continuum of care in various communities. Such resource and service integration problems can be expected to limit the impact of case management and referral service programs (McBride et al., 1999).

A STUDY OF PRELIMINARY SCREENING

The subject of this study, a Family Empowerment Intervention (FEI), was implemented as part of the Youth Support Project (YSP) funded by the National Institute on Drug Abuse (NIDA). The YSP operated out of the Hillsborough County (Tampa, Florida) Juvenile Assessment Center (JAC). All youths entering the project were first processed at the JAC. The YSP was overlaid upon existing JAC operations. As part of our ongoing research, we conducted a study of the JAC assessors' preliminary screening results, the assessor staff's service recommendations, and service utilization outcomes of 143 youths processed at the JAC between 1994 and 1996 who subsequently entered the YSP. The analyses focused on the relationships among youths' potential problems identified during the JAC preliminary screening process, assessor indications of problem areas, and assessor recommendations for follow-up services.

Several statistically significant relationships were found between identified youth problems and JAC case managers' or assessors' evaluations and recommendations:

1. A positive relationship between ever receiving mental health treatment and the general problem identified by the case manager or assessor
2. Positive relationships between past year reported frequency of alcohol and marijuana/hashish use and
   a. assessor-identified substance abuse problems
   b. referral to in-depth assessment
   c. referral to a JAC-based TASC/Delinquency Assessment Team (DAT) staff member
3. A positive relationship between the youths' scores on the Problem Oriented Screening Instrument for Teenagers (POSIT) (Rahdert, 1991) and the case manager's or assessor's identification of family abuse problems
4. A negative relationship between ever receiving substance abuse treatment and assessor-identified vocational skill and gang problems

Overall, nine of these relationships were found to be statistically significant, compared to less than two that, on average, could be expected to be produced by chance alone. At the same time, however, the magnitude of the significant relationships was modest. The largest correlation ($r = .55$) was between reported lifetime frequency of marijuana/hashish use and assessor-identified substance abuse problems; the average, absolute value of the significant correlations was .31.

Experience indicated that 55 percent of all youths brought to the Tampa JAC were processed during the 3 to 11 p.m. shift. The staff working this shift is limited and often serves twenty to thirty youths in various stages of the JAC registration and preliminary screening process; youths often get "backed-up" and have to wait to be processed. Given this situation, we anticipated that the quality of staff assessments and youth responses to the preliminary screening questions would decline during this shift. We examined this issue by comparing reported past year alcohol and marijuana use, reported ever receiving mental health or substance misuse treatment, and responses to the POSIT for youths processed during the 3 to 11 p.m. shift versus other shifts (i.e., 7 a.m. to 3 p.m. and 11 p.m. to 7 a.m.).

Relatedly, the three shifts were compared in regard to assessor-identified problem areas requiring follow-up. Analysis indicated that youths processed during the 3 to 11 p.m. shift reported significantly less involvement in alcohol and marijuana use than those processed during the other shifts. Accordingly, processing shift (the 3 to 11 p.m. shift versus the two other shifts) was included in our further analyses of these data.

Mutual relationships were found among assessor evaluations and recommendations, processing shift, and the youths' demographic characteristics. Accordingly, partial correlations were obtained between the youths' substance use/psychosocial problems and assessor evaluations and recommendations, controlling for processing shift and the youths' demographic factors. The results indicated that, with two exceptions, the statistically significant relationships remained significant. The two exceptions were the association between assessor recommendations for youths to receive in-depth assessments and the youths' reported past year frequency of use of alcohol and marijuana/hashish.

Fifty-six of the 143 youths (39 percent) were recommended for in-depth assessment by TASC/DAT staff. A letter was sent to each of the parents/guardians of the youths offering to provide a free in-depth assessment. Information was collected on the outcomes of some of these referrals, but follow-up or outcome information could not be located for twenty-four (43 percent) of the fifty-six cases. The results indicated that twenty-seven (84 percent) of the thirty-two clients or their families with follow-up information did not respond to the letter from TASC/DAT staff. Two clients contacted staff, who thought the client did not need an in-depth assessment, and the parent of one youth called to say her child would receive services elsewhere. Only two (6 percent) of the thirty-two visited the TASC/DAT office, at which point they were referred to an assessment service. Thus, very few clients or their families were engaged in the assessment process.

Although significant associations were found between assessor recommendations for specific services and the preliminarily screened youths' reported alcohol/other drug and mental health problems, the magnitude of these relationships was in the low-to-moderate range. The results highlight that assessor staff needed initial and ongoing training and experience in identifying potential psychosocial functioning and substance use problems among processed youths and in making appropriate service recommendations for them. This training should reflect an appreciation of the sociocultural diversity existing within the population of youths entering the juvenile justice system, and it should seek to provide a more complete understanding of their problems and service needs. Ongoing research at the JAC highlighted the importance of this work (Dembo et al., 1995).

The failure of most youths or their families to follow through with the recommended in-depth assessments, however, points to the very serious need to develop more effective ways for involving youths in needed follow-up services. The development of effective engagement strategies and intervention services for multiple-problem families, such as many families whose youngsters are often processed at the JAC, presents considerable challenges to service providers. Our study highlighted that few youths with an indicated need for substance misuse or mental health services become involved in these services. A major loss point occurred in families not following through on the invitation to participate in a free in-depth assessment—an experience that repeatedly occurs in service delivery efforts involving youths in the juvenile justice system.

Low-cost in-home interventions for these youths and their families would be an optimal way to involve them in needed services. The Family Empowerment Intervention is an example of this kind of service. Although demanding, such interventions hold great promise of remediating the problems of troubled youths and their families, improving family functioning, and reducing the flow of these youths deeper into the juvenile justice system. Providing in-home intervention services constructively gets around problems many families experience in accessing needed services: location of services in areas geographically distant from their homes, transportation problems, and the need to have neighbors or baby-sitters look after very young children while other family members access services (Dembo, Schmeidler, et al., 1997).

THE IMPORTANCE OF FAMILY INTERVENTIONS WITH AN ECOLOGICAL FOCUS

It is now widely accepted that to be effective, intervention programs for youths must involve the family (Kumpfer and Alvarado, 1998). Many youths' problems develop within a family context, and their troubled behavior often reflects issues and problems parents/ guardians and other family members are experiencing. For example, one in four American children has been exposed to alcohol abuse at home (Grant, 2000). In addition, many juvenile arrestees reside in households in which a parent/guardian or other family member is experiencing other drug abuse, mental health problems, or some involvement with the justice system (Dembo, Seeberger, et al., 2000). Intervention programs that work with the family, and that seek to empower parents within the family and strengthen their ability to relate more effectively in their communities and with agencies and institutions affecting their lives (e.g., schools), have the greatest chance of effecting significant and lasting changes (Alexander and Parsons, 1982; Henggeler et al., 1994).

A number of intervention efforts focusing on family preservation and informed by an ecological systems view (Bronfenbrenner, 1979) have been implemented in various parts of the country (e.g., Szapocznik and Kurtines, 1989; Rahdert and Czechowicz, 1995; Kumpfer and Alvarado, 1998). For example, multisystemic therapy (MST) has been found successful in addressing the needs of juvenile offenders and their families (Henggeler and Borduin, 1990; Henggeler et al., 1993, 1994). Clinical trials of MST have involved service delivery at community mental health centers. Trained therapists have provided services to four to six "at-risk juveniles" and their families for as long as four to five months. The family preservation focus of MST seeks to "empower parents to restructure their environments in ways that promote development" by strengthening their parental competencies (Henggeler et al., 1994:21). From the perspective of structural family therapy, an essential first step is to focus on the parents in order to restructure the family and establish parental control. A second goal is to teach the parents how to use agencies and services, including schools, more effectively (Henggeler et al., 1994).

Functional family therapy (Alexander and Parsons, 1982) has been found effective in treating juveniles eleven to eighteen years of age who are involved in alcohol or other drug abuse or delinquent behavior, and in reducing justice and other service costs in serving these juveniles. A wide range of trained interventionists, working in one- or two-person teams, provide from eight to twenty-six hours of in-home services to referred juveniles and their families. The services involve five phases: engagement, motivation, assessment, behavioral change, and generalization.

Originally developed to address the needs of Cuban families in Miami, brief strategic family therapy (BSFT) has been found to be effective in improving family functioning and redirecting the behavior of troubled youths in more positive directions (Szapocznik and Kurtines, 1989, 1993; Robbins and Szapocznik, 2000). This intervention is informed by a systems view of families, family structure and patterns of interaction, and strategy (interventions that are designed to move families toward desired goals). Professional therapists deliver services at their offices and in the homes of families receiving BSFT services. The BSFT has come to incorporate bicultural effectiveness training, a psychoeducational component, a One-Person Family Therapy variant, a structural strategic systems engagement component, and an ecosystems adaptation of BSFT (Szapocznik et al., 1990). The BSFT approach has also been adapted to serve a broader representation of Hispanic families from Latin America and, more recently, African-American families.

Although the above family interventions have shown promising results (Henggeler et al., 1993; Kumpfer and Alvarado, 1998; Robbins and Szapocznik, 2000) in the aggregate, they include several features that may limit their attractiveness to budget-conscious service providers. First, a number of these interventions involve trained therapists, which increases the cost of the services. Second, sometimes these intervention services are delivered in a therapist's office, some distance from the families receiving them, which can affect families' engagement and involvement in them.

In some cases, there have been difficulties in evaluating these interventions, which limits the generalizability of their results. Some interventions reflect more "laboratory ideal" programs than "in life" services. That is, evaluations of some interventions have excluded data from project personnel depending on the quality of their work (i.e., project management thought they were not carrying out the intervention as intended) (Scherer et al., 1998). This is an unfair assessment of the real world of service delivery. Relatedly, few of these interventions document ongoing efforts to ensure the integrity of the intervention over time. *Integrity of the intervention* refers to continuing efforts to ensure that the services are being delivered in the manner in which they were intended. This is an important consideration in real-world service delivery, where clinical and intervention staff turnover is commonplace. Further, interventions may have been developed to address the needs of specific cultural groups or developed and implemented in different parts of the country. Although these interventions may be highly successful in working with families from these groups in specific areas, their effectiveness among other groups may not yet be firmly established.

The Family Empowerment Intervention described in this report was informed by the previously described intervention services, particularly the MST. The goal of the FEI is to improve family functioning by empowering parents. It was anticipated that by empowering parents the behavior of the juvenile offenders involved in the intervention would become more prosocial. The FEI is an intensive, systems-oriented, and structural intervention delivered in the home. A field consultant assigned to the family meets with the family three times a week for approximately ten weeks. Each family meeting lasts one hour. All household members (i.e., those living under the same roof as the youth) are expected to be present for these meetings. The diverse groups of youths receiving FEI services included relatively nonserious offenders (i.e., arrested for minor misdemeanor offenses, such as retail theft) with no previous arrests as well as youths charged with more serious offenses (e.g., burglary). As discussed in Chapter 2, multiple, ongoing efforts were made to ensure the integrity of the intervention.

Youth and family enrollment in the project was voluntary. After youths and their families had agreed to participate in the Youth Support Project and an in-depth baseline interview had been completed, youths and their families were randomly assigned to the FEI group or placed in a control group, the Extended Services Intervention (ESI) group. Families in the ESI group were able to benefit from an extensive resource file developed by YSP staff to gain referrals to other agencies in the community. This resource system enabled project research staff to provide families with information about different community agencies, and staff members assisted families in obtaining appropriate referrals to meet their needs. FEI families were able to use this resource as well.

One distinctive feature of the FEI was that families were served by paraprofessional field consultants. The consultants were not trained therapists, although they were trained by, and performed their work under the direction of, licensed clinicians. The choice of paraprofessionals was based on a cost-effectiveness argument and is supported by experimental research indicating that, at least for some treatments, paraprofessionals produce outcomes that are better than those produced under control conditions and similar to those involving professional therapists (Christensen and Jacobson, 1994; Weisz et al., 1995). Further, by requiring less previous therapy training, the FEI, if proven to be effective, is more likely to be funded than more costly alternatives given the financial limitations facing most service delivery agencies. Many treatment programs face considerable financial challenges in providing quality services to troubled youths and their families, which often precludes the extensive use of professional therapists. For example, while MST has been found to be effective with noninstitutionalized offenders, this family service tends to be costly (approximately $6,000 per family) because trained therapists usually provide the intervention. Other effective, but more economical, family intervention services are needed to meet the needs of jurisdictions that lack the resources to implement MST. The FEI costs less than $1,200 per family.

Another distinctive feature of the FEI was the commitment of staff to work with youths who moved to another family setting during the course of the intervention. For example, if the juvenile receiving FEI services moved from his mother's household to that of his grandmother, the field consultant would implement the FEI in the grandmother's home. A further feature of the FEI involved working with youths who were incarcerated. If a youth involved in the intervention was placed in a juvenile detention center or in county jail, the family meetings were held in that setting. This arrangement benefited the youth and family by enabling them to continue to move toward completion of the intervention. It also provided a resource to help the youth make the transition back into the community.

CRITERIA FOR EVALUATING INTERVENTION PROGRAMS

The Center for the Study and Prevention of Violence (1999) has established a set of widely accepted criteria for determining the effectiveness of intervention programs. These include (1) a rigorous study design, (2) evidence of the program's impact in producing positive outcomes, (3) evidence of sustained effects, and (4) multisite replications. *Rigorous study design* refers to the use of random assignment, which usually provides the best opportunity to assess confidently the impact of an intervention program. (Ideally, this should include blind outcome assessment.) The distinction between evidence of *producing positive outcomes* and *sustained effects* is very important. Intervention programs can often demonstrate success in improving psychosocial functioning or in reducing recidivism (e.g., new arrests or convictions) while juveniles are involved in the program or for a short period afterward. Many fewer programs can document continued beneficial effects for periods longer than one year after the intervention. In the Youth Support Project, depending on the year in which a juvenile entered the project, we tracked the youths' (1) recidivism from twelve months up to forty-eight months following random assignment to the FEI or ESI, and (2) psychosocial functioning for twelve to thirty-six months after completing their baseline interviews.

ORGANIZATION OF REPORT

Chapter 2 discusses the theoretical foundations and clinical practices of the Family Empowerment Intervention. We review the theoretical background of the FEI, its goals and intervention strategies, phases of the intervention, engaging families and moving them through the FEI, the selection of field consultants and their roles and training, the roles and responsibilities of key supervisory personnel, clinical policies, and efforts to ensure the integrity of the FEI.

Chapter 3 describes the procedures used to select youths and families for enrollment into the Youth Support Project. Data-collection strategies and their results are also presented. Descriptive information is provided on participating youths' sociodemographic characteristics at entry; educational and previous treatment experiences; self-reports and the results of hair testing for alcohol/other drug use; official records of delinquency and abuse-neglect histories; and self-report data on their physical and sexual abuse histories, other areas of emotional/psychological functioning, and their delinquent behavior.

Chapter 4 presents the results of our short- (twelve months) and long-term (up to forty-eight months) outcome studies of the impact of the FEI on the youths' delinquent behavior. We report on our analyses of official record and self-report information on delinquency and crime.

Chapter 5 reports the results of our detailed analyses of the short-term and long-term impact of the FEI on the youths' drug use, as indicated by their self-reports of this behavior and by their hair test results.

Chapter 6 presents the results of our short- and long-term studies of the impact of the FEI on the youths' emotional/psychological functioning. The discussion focuses on findings from administering a well-established inventory, the SCL-90-R (Symptom Check List-90-Revised) (Derogatis, 1983). The chapter also includes a discussion of the relationship between involvement in the FEI and the youths' reported (1) satisfaction with their families, and (2) communication with their mothers.

Chapter 7 summarizes what we learned from the Youth Support Project. We review what the results of our various analyses indicate regarding the short-term impact and sustained effects of the FEI. We also estimate the direct cost savings for the juvenile system associated with implementing the FEI. The research and policy implications of our work are also presented. In this context, we review achievements and challenges experienced in developing, implementing, and evaluating the FEI. Our focus is on lessons learned and steps to be taken in providing effective, cost-efficient services to high-risk youths and their families.

Chapter 2

Overview of the Family Empowerment Intervention

In this chapter, we present a detailed description of the Family Empowerment Intervention (FEI), which was implemented and evaluated as part of the Youth Support Project (YSP). The following topics are covered: theoretical foundations; goals; structural intervention strategies; phases of the intervention; categories of families served by the FEI; engaging and moving families through the FEI to graduation; the role, qualifications, and training of the field consultants who delivered the intervention; the roles and responsibilities of key supervisory personnel; clinical policies; efforts to ensure the integrity of intervention services; and implementing the FEI.

THEORETICAL FOUNDATIONS

The FEI is an in-home program for delinquent youths and their families. It offers highly interactive, experiential activities that facilitate a positive emotional climate within the family, revitalize the family's natural strengths, and improve the interpersonal skills of family members. In addition, many of the FEI activities facilitate development of a more effective, adaptive, and workable family structure. The FEI is informed by four theoretical approaches: systemic, structural, transgenerational, and psychoeducational.

Systemic

According to a systemic approach, family members are interconnected and interdependent units of a larger system. Their thoughts, beliefs, and behaviors can be understood as part of an interactive pattern in which each member influences, evokes responses from, and/or responds to someone else (Bateson et al., 1956; Bateson, 1979). The interactive patterns of behavior are viewed as predictable, cyclical, and self-sustaining. They are repetitive actions that maintain a familiar way of operating.

The systemic perspective does not view one family member as having "the problem." Rather, the problem is understood as emerging from the "social field" (Hoffman, 1981) in which it occurs (Haley, 1976). It shows something about the larger picture in the family. Focusing on the social unit, the interactive pattern in the family rather than the individual, can move families away from blaming, scapegoating, or looking for a simple cause. It also raises different, more interesting concerns: What influences do family members have over each other through behaviors, conversations, and nonverbal exchanges? How do family members regulate closeness and distance? How are anger, disagreement, and conflict managed? How are rules and roles established and maintained? In what ways is the family affected by social forces (schools, social service agencies, law enforcement, media)? What are the family legacies, rituals, and myths that influence current family interactions? Questions such as these help identify the depth and complexity of everyday family life.

Structural

The structural approach emphasizes family organization and interactive processes as key concepts in understanding a family (Minuchin, 1974, 1981, 1984). Family dysfunction is understood as a reflection of difficulties in these areas. Following are the central elements of the structural perspective:

- *Hierarchy* denotes the organization of power in the family. Who makes the decisions about finances? Household chores? Curfews? Who do the children go to for permission to sleep at a friend's house? How are discipline and limit setting managed in the family? In well-functioning families, the adult caregivers are considered the "executive branch" and have the mechanisms by which to wield appropriate power. Troubled families are characterized by inconsistent, chaotic, and unpredictable organization of power. Moreover, in those families, the child(ren) exert more power than is appropriate. For example, a twelve-year-old son

who has been "parentified" by his single parent is required to act
as a coparent to a younger sibling.

- *Subsystems* are smaller units within a family system. These
units are well defined and have their own specific roles and
functions (i.e., parental subsystem and sibling subsystem).

- *Boundaries* are the invisible lines among family members, subsystems, and the larger community. The term also refers to rules,
expectations, and roles that define members of these groups. Examples include such everyday occurrences as knocking on a
parent's or sibling's bedroom door before entering, calling home
if more than thirty minutes late, or asking twenty-four hours in
advance for permission to sleep at a friend's house. Boundaries
strongly affect the nature and health of family subsystems. If
boundaries are excessively rigid, impermeable barriers between
members exist. If they are excessively blurred, a lack of clarity
is present. Healthy boundaries foster a good balance between
self-differentiation and mutuality. Also, healthy boundaries are
created in response to the changing developmental needs of
family members.

  Since healthy boundaries are essential to a well-functioning
family hierarchy, FEI interventions and interactions by field
consultants encourage strengthening the "executive branch" of
the family (e.g., staff address the parents as Mr., Ms., or Mrs.,
unless they request first names; ask "permission" from parents
to make a directive or a suggestion to the client youth; and request that parents sit together during the meetings). Each of
these interactions relays the message to the parent(s), "We respect your position in this family. You are the head(s) of this
household." By doing so, the field consultant communicates
positive regard for the parent(s) and models this for the children.

- *Alignments* are the ways in which family members join together
or oppose one another. For example, Mr. Rodriguez would tend
to align himself with the client youth, Luisa, when she broke a
family rule such as violating curfew or failing to do chores. He
would do so by making excuses for, or ignoring, her behavior.
Frequently, the Rodriguezes would argue about "his always taking up for Luisa." The field consultant assisted Mr. and Mrs. Rodriguez in presenting a "united front" when their daughter
behaved inappropriately. This represented a more constructive
and generationally appropriate alignment.

- A *triangulation* is an alliance that has a negative impact on another member of the family. These alliances are dysfunctional in that they disrupt family organization and create inappropriate boundaries. The Rodriguez family represents a triangulation of an allied father and daughter "against" the mother.

Transgenerational

The transgenerational perspective understands the family as comprising an entire kinship network of at least three generations. The current family system is profoundly influenced by its history and family legacy. In order to fully understand and appreciate what happens in the family, it is often helpful to understand the generational context. What were the significant issues in previous generations—alcoholism? chronic illness? sudden death of a spouse? How have these life events affected family members? In what ways do unresolved experiences and struggles get passed on to the current generation?

Families can be viewed as repeating themselves over time. What happens in one generation will often get played out in another one. Although there are variations of behaviors and "scripts," the inherent issues and themes remain the same. These themes influence member's actions, expectations, assumptions, and roles within the family. These recurring patterns become "family echoes." Two examples follow:

- The client youth, Isaac, was described by his mother as "just like my daddy . . . lazy and without one whit of sense." How do these expectations affect mother's behavior toward Isaac? To what extent is a self-fulfilling prophecy occurring? How has mother's difficult relationship with her own father affected her style of parenting? To what extent do her negative feelings about her dad get expressed through her interactions with her son?
- During the second meeting, the father informed the field consultant that the client youth's mother committed suicide when she (Gina) was three years old "but since Gina was too young to remember her mother, it has never been discussed." This information provides the consultant with valuable insight into how this family deals with grief and pain. What other issues are avoided by the family? How does this family manage change and loss?

In what ways has Gina dealt with her mother's death? How have Gina and the family dealt with the absence of a mother in the family?

A structured format for learning about a family's generational context is provided by the genogram. Similar to a family tree, a genogram records information about family members and structure over at least three generations. Genograms are usually associated with Bowen's family systems theory (Bowen, 1978; McGoldrick and Gerson, 1985), but they may be applied in a wide range of clinical orientations. A genogram provides a visual picture of the family; it represents the family gestalt. Genograms depict recurring family difficulties (legal and community involvement, substance abuse, physical or sexual abuse); family strengths and achievements (escaping poverty, graduating high school); historical events (relocations, deaths, long absences); demographics (birth dates, education, chronic illnesses); and predominant familial beliefs, myths, and legacies ("The Thompson boys have this anger streak. It's just the way we've always been. We don't take any disrespect from anybody.").

The field consultant constructs the genogram with the family during the first or second meeting. The reasons for doing so are threefold. First, it offers an excellent opportunity for the field consultant to rapidly engage with members in a nonthreatening manner. Second, it shifts the focus from the client youth to the family system. By doing so, family members can "get the big picture" and begin to think differently about their current difficulties. Third, it provides the consultant with valuable information about the family system in a timely manner.

Families often acknowledge that constructing a genogram together provides a rich opportunity to learn about one another's personal stories and shared family history. Genograms are a powerful vehicle for mapping the evolution of the family and strengthening bonds between members.

Psychoeducational

The family's acquisition of successful life-management and interpersonal skills is a core FEI objective. Thus, the psychoeducational model, which emphasizes skill building and behavioral change, is used. This model embraces a wide spectrum of approaches that are primarily cognitive-behavioral and instructional. Psychoeducational approaches are used to improve communication, conflict-resolution, anger-management, and problem-solving skills within the family. Psychoeducational approaches are also used for developing better social skills at school and in the community. This model emphasizes role playing, homework assignments, and other practical strategies that promote desired behavioral change.

GOALS

Deriving from the theoretical foundations of this intervention are its nine specific goals. These goals should be regarded as separate yet interrelated objectives that together strengthen family structure and functioning (Cervenka, Dembo, and Brown, 1996).

1. Restore the family hierarchy (parents > children).
2. Restructure boundaries between parents and children.
3. Encourage parents to take greater responsibility for family functioning.
4. Strengthen family structure through implementation of rules and consequences.
5. Enhance parenting skills.
6. Have parents set limits, expectations, and rules that increase the likelihood the client youth's behavior will improve.
7. Improve communication skills among all family members and the ability to have fun together.
8. Improve problem-solving skills, particularly in the client youth.
9. When needed, connect the family to other systems (school, church, community activities)—"system fit."

STRUCTURAL INTERVENTION STRATEGIES

The FEI is described in an FEI manual, which consists of two complementary documents: an implementation manual and an activities manual. The implementation manual provides the theoretical foundations for the FEI, together with the policies and practices involved in carrying out the intervention. The activities manual presents specific games, artistic projects, and exercises in which family members can engage to facilitate achieving the goals of the intervention. The activities manual evolved from our early experience in implementing the FEI, which indicated that many of the families we worked with did not respond well to verbal interaction and sharing of feelings and information. The various activities often bring to light issues the families are confronting in a manner they can directly understand. We have found that field consultants often carry the activities manual with them in the field to plan specific activities for family meetings or to use in setting up or providing instructions for specific games, exercises, and the like. The following is an example of a game from the FEI activities manual.

The game "Inside, Outside" is an exercise to increase bondedness among family members. It is an enjoyable and nonthreatening way to deepen understanding of self and others, appreciate individual differences, and strengthen closeness. Also, this activity is a powerful way for family members to see themselves through the eyes of others. How does my mother view me? In what ways does my "public" self accurately represent my "private" self? Inside, Outside facilitates self-disclosure, open communication, and building self-esteem.

- *Purpose:* To explore how family members are perceived by one another in contrast to how each member sees his or her own self.
- *Type:* Nonverbal activity, verbal follow-up.
- *Materials:* Large paper bags (one for each member), a variety of magazines, tape, markers, and scissors.
- *Instructions:* Give each person some magazines, a bag, and scissors. Ask them to cut out pictures, words, and phrases that describe or represent who they are and place them in the bag. When that exercise is completed, each person writes his or her name on the outside of the bag. These individual bags are then passed around. Next, family members cut out pictures, words, phrases that describe/represent other family members. These items are taped on the outside of the respective bags. Each person can then discuss the contrast between his or her "inside" view and the views of the family members "outside." Toward the end of the intervention, the family members are encouraged to revisit how they saw themselves, how others saw them, and how things have changed.
- *Goals:* 5, 6, 7, 8 (see p. 20).

The interventions used in the FEI are primarily strategic in nature. They focus on the here and now with an emphasis on modifying repetitive, dysfunctional interactive patterns. The interventions are structured, action oriented, behavioral, and designed to challenge, shift, interrupt, or strengthen and highlight family processes. Within the context of these interventions, the field consultant utilizes six interactional processes: engaging, joining, tracking, enactment, circular questioning, and reframing.

Engaging

Engaging is an interpersonal process whereby the field consultant connects with the family in an empathetic and positive manner. This increases the likelihood that the family will accept the field consultant and become actively involved with the program. The engagement process is one of the most important aspects of the introduction of the field consultant to the family. Successful engagement heightens the family members' sense of being genuinely respected, acknowledged, and understood. This early connection communicates to family members that their involvement in the intervention will be positive and rewarding. The genogram is an excellent vehicle for engaging family members. Using the genogram, the field consultant is able to ask everyone questions, facilitate positive conversation, and show interest in the family's history. More important, he or she establishes the emotional tone for the helping relationship. The field consultant sends the message, "I am interested in your family. I want to know you and it's important that you know one another." For more active, less verbally expressive families, the field consultant might postpone using the genogram and use a puzzle or game. These activities can strengthen the link between the field consultant and more experientially oriented families. This willingness to engage a family in terms of "where they are at" builds trust and expresses positive regard.

The engagement process continues throughout the intervention. It plays out differently at different times, but its purpose remains the same—to connect with the family in a meaningful way. Although some activities are used for engagement, there is no substitute for an empathetic, present-centered field consultant. The quality of "self" is the most important key to successful engagement.

Joining

Joining is another form of engagement with the family; however, it typically denotes a process whereby the field consultant specifically connects with one person or subsystem in the family. It is a way of shifting, interrupting, or strengthening an interactional pattern. For instance, the client youth, Elise, is an only child. Frequently, her parents argue about rules and expectations, and Elise feels caught in the middle of a power struggle. As a way of joining, a field consultant who is an only child could acknowledge his or her own experience. The field consultant might interrupt the parent's arguing by saying to the father, "Boy, I sure remember being caught in the middle of my mother and father. That wasn't much fun! How do you imagine Elise might feel right now?" This intervention has three benefits. First, the field consultant joins with the client youth by communicating, "Hey, I know how you may feel right now." Second, it invites the father to empathize with the client youth. Third, it opens the door for a very different conversation, thereby interrupting the negative, repetitive interactional pattern.

Tracking

Tracking is a strategy whereby the field consultant identifies significant symbolic expression communicated by family members. For example, in a "family portrait" drawing, a mother drew herself in the corner of the paper. Upon exploration, the mother acknowledged that she frequently felt like going to the corner when family conflict emerged. This metaphor became a meaningful, yet playful, theme that helped this family resolve important issues around anger and conflict. This metaphor enabled the mother to communicate ideas, thoughts, and feelings in a safe, indirect, and creative way. Metaphors offer powerful ways to describe the usual in an unusual manner.

Because many FEI activities encourage symbolic expression, tracking is a particularly valuable process. It highlights and clarifies the individual language of experience, thus enabling members to gain insight into themselves and other members. Families now have an opportunity to gain a fresh perspective and develop new ways to respond to one another.

Enactment

Enactment is a process in which family members are instructed to interact in their typical manner and then are shown how to modify their interactions in more positive ways. For example, Dean, aged thirteen, frequently nags his mother when she sets limits about curfews and friends. After several minutes of this, his father starts to yell at him. Name calling, arguing, and fighting ensue. The enactment follows: Step 1: The field consultant asks each member to act out his or her usual part of "the family dance." Step 2: Family members are asked to become "observers" of their interaction. What could they have done differently? How could Mom or Dad respond differently? What might be other ways for Dean to deal with his frustration? Step 3: The family is instructed to role-play this new interaction. Also, having families review a particular segment of a videotape recorded at a previous family meeting offers an excellent opportunity for enactment.

Circular Questioning

Based on systems theory, *circular questioning* is a style of inquiry designed to reveal patterns and connections. Circular questioning invites family members to reflect on issues, explore individual perceptions, and address concerns in a highly interactive manner. It is based on the view that behaviors are systemic, interactional, repetitive, and predictable. Actions and beliefs of family members are interrelated, each person influencing the other. These interactional patterns are cyclical and exist as feedback loops within the system. People are more accustomed to thinking in linear causality terms, that is, one event causes the next in a stimulus-response manner. Hence, A would cause B and B would cause C. Circular causality would view all the events at one time causing each of the events at a later time. It suggests that there are forces moving in several directions simultaneously, not simply a single event caused by another.

Circular questioning focuses attention on family connections rather than on individual problems: Who in the family gets most upset? How do other members typically respond to this person? What does Mom do when Dad worries about your sister? What does Susie do when Alex has a tantrum? In what ways does your stepfather show you he really cares about your mother? By asking several family members the same question about a concern, one is able to probe more deeply without being overly confrontational or harsh. The field consultant gently "opens the door" to explore the personal meaning of events and relationships within the family. The benefits of circular questioning include opening up family members to new information and understanding of themselves and others (these new perceptions offer members possibilities for innovative and more positive solutions); increasing empathy; breaking repetitive, negative interactional patterns; and communicating to the family that the field consultant views each member's perceptions as unique, valuable, and meaningful. By doing so, the field consultant strengthens a sense of family empowerment and decreases an overreliance on the consultant as the "family expert."

Reframing

Reframing is the technique of relabeling a behavior by putting it into a new, more positive perspective. For example, a stubborn child might be described as focused and persistent. Or a father's criticism of his son might be a sign of the father's best way of expressing his interest and care. Chronic fighting between a mother and daughter is relabeled as an indicator of how "really plugged into one another they must be." Reframing offers members a position of power and competency, rather than deficiency, in dealing with family challenges. The primary objectives of reframing are to provoke a more positive reaction to the behavior, help individuals view intentions and actions in a fresh way, open up the system to creative change, and show that there is more than one way to see a particular situation.

PHASES OF THE INTERVENTION

The FEI is designed to proceed through four phases: introduction, consultation, family work, and graduation. Ideally, the field consultant meets with the family three times a week for ten weeks.

Phase 1: Introduction

Phase 1 (session 1 or 1-2) is characterized by the introduction of the field consultant and all family members involved, a description of the intervention and supervision design, a review of the intervention procedures (including videotaping or audiotaping family meetings) and timing, and responses to any questions the family may have about the program.

Content

Introduction of everyone present
Description of the intervention by the field consultant
Introduction of taping program for supervision
Signatures of all present on taping-approval form
Set-up of audio/videotaping
Presentation of supervision requirement
Questions posed and answered about the YSP and the FEI
Introduction of a genogram format
Construction of the first genogram
Inquiry as to family style of interacting
Review of session(s)
Establishment of at least two additional appointments, repetition of ideal of three meetings a week for ten weeks

Field Consultant Guidelines

Videotape family meetings.
Use last names with Mr., Ms., or Mrs. for parent generation unless instructed otherwise by them (first session, try to retain formality).
Have parents introduce children whenever possible.
Shake everyone's hand, or make close contact with each member, bearing in mind cultural differences in "space" and greeting.
Observe interaction in response to a new person (field consultant).
Ask what expectations/fears the family members had in letting a new person into their home for many weeks.
Consider feeling tone in the family.

Identify all family members who live in the home.

Try to identify other significant members of the family circle.

Try, whenever possible, to reframe the focus from the client youth to the whole family (describe FEI as many times as needed).

Make eye contact with everyone present at least once.

Keep FEI goals in mind.

Present a positive, hopeful picture to the family before leaving.

Have signed taping form in field notes when leaving.

Obtain agreement as to next meeting time and agenda.

Phase 2: Consultation

Phase 2 (ideally sessions 2-3 through 9-12) is characterized by inquiry and participation by the field consultant and demonstration of the methods used for sharing/asking. The field consultant conducts the activities.

Content

Review of prior sessions

Round-robins
- Family roles and rules
- Family communication
- Generational differences and hierarchy
- Boundaries and relationships

Genogram and family picture construction
- Discussion of family themes and history

Use of paper and pencil, drawings, landscapes with stickers, games, and the like to exemplify family feelings and interactions; "who in the family . . ." and other tools for family inquiry

Use of communication games, puzzles, and the like, to assess family styles and interaction and determine how they can best work together

Behavioral methods: positive outcomes, "catch 'em being good," charting

Discussion of discipline, compliance, and consequences

Anger-management techniques

Goal setting—individual and family

Review at end of each session; repetition of what has occurred

At each session, establishment of at least two additional appointments, repetition of ideal of three times a week, ideally for ten weeks

Field Consultant Guidelines

Arrive at each session with a planned agenda of activities.

Introduce activities/agendas that include fun/positive feelings.

Videotape family meetings.

Arrange seating by generations to establish hierarchy.

Start with statement about the last session ("I thought about what you said . . .") and a question about the family's reaction ("What were you thinking about at last time's discussion of . . . ?") to ensure continuity and to "link" the sessions in their minds.

Keep FEI goals in mind.

Start by taking the lead, gradually giving the leadership to the family.

Refer to the genogram information at every session.

Be sure each person in the family has "air time."

Make eye contact with everyone present at least once.

Present a positive, hopeful picture to the family before leaving.

Obtain agreement as to next meeting time and agenda.

Phase 3: Family Work

Phase 3 (ideally sessions 10-13 through 27) is characterized by the family members taking the lead in reorganizing ways of communicating, relating, and thinking about family functioning.

Content

Workbook activities on behavioral charting, expectations, and so on

Family reviews genograms/family themes together; little field consultant prompting

Family members set personal goals and prepare written statements where possible

Family sets goals for family as a unit and prepares written statements where possible

Family decides how to reach new family goals and how to make life more pleasant and interesting for each other

Family works on issues of roles/responsibilities

Family sets rewards for instances in which responsibilities are met

Family sets consequences for failed attempts at being responsible

Family discusses generational expectations and hierarchy

Family solves problems together

Field consultant may provide tasks, games, and constructions

Family practices communication with each other in dyads, triads, and generational groups

Client youth describes his or her contact with the justice system

Client youth works out plans with family for constructive activity

Client youth receives support from family for change

Review at end of each session to repeat what has occurred

At each session, establishment of at least two additional appointments, repetition of ideal of three times per week, ideally for ten weeks

Family establishes agenda for the next meeting

Field Consultant Guidelines

Videotape family meeting.

Start with statement about the last session ("I thought about what you said . . .") and a question about the family's reaction ("What were you thinking about at last time's discussion of . . . ?") to ensure continuity and to "link" the sessions in their minds.

Have the agenda in mind for each session.

Suggest activities appropriate to the agenda at the beginning of the session, allow family to choose.

Be sure the family members have the goal areas in mind as they work.

When a family gets "stuck," suggest discussion of being stuck and how to get out of it.

Provide positive feedback every time initiative is taken by a family member.

Model techniques of reflecting, responding, fairness in interaction.

Show a videotape from earlier sessions for change recognition.
Make eye contact with everyone present at least once.
Focus attention upon positive planning for client youth and others.
Present a positive, hopeful picture to the family before leaving.
Obtain agreement as to next meeting time and agenda.

Phase 4: Graduation

Phase 4 (ideally sessions 28-30) is characterized by review of the intervention and preparation for separation from the FEI. It takes place after the field consultant and supervisor have agreed that the family has met the goals of the intervention.

Content

Discussion of change and changes
Overview of goals to be achieved over time
Review of earlier videotapes for confirmation of change
Final activities: planning the party
Party and celebration

Field Consultant Guidelines

Start with statement about the last session ("I thought about what you said . . .") and a question about the family's reaction ("What were you thinking about at last time's discussion of . . . ?") to ensure continuity and to "link" the sessions in their minds.
Have an agenda for each final session: review, reframe, refresh.
Videotape family meetings.
Introduce a "future genogram": Where does the family want to be next year, the year after?
Help the family set up methods of communicating after the intervention is completed.
Review progress made over the course of the intervention.
Talk about partings and saying good-bye.
Provide positive feedback every time initiative is taken by family member.

Model techniques of reflecting, responding, fairness in interaction.

Show a videotape from earlier sessions for change recognition.

Make eye contact with everyone present at least once.

Focus attention upon positive planning for client youth and others.

Present a positive, hopeful picture to the family before leaving.

Say good-bye to each family member at the party, giving each positive feedback about his or her role in the project.

Remind the family to have fun together.

Present the Certificate of Completion ("diploma").

CATEGORIES OF FAMILIES SERVED BY THE FEI

Based on our experience implementing the FEI, we have identified four categories of families:

- *Active Families:* Currently being served by a field consultant.
- *Graduation Provisionally Delayed/ "On-Hold" Families:* Incarceration or other family circumstance prevents full participation, but there is an expectation that the family will complete the intervention and graduate.
- *Graduated Families:* Completed intervention.
- *Inactive/Closed Families:* Families that have not completed the intervention despite the activities listed in the section on Clinical Policies and for whom there is little or no expectation that they will complete the intervention and graduate.

INVOLVING FAMILIES AND MOVING THEM THROUGH THE FEI TO GRADUATION

Many of the families with which we work are difficult to engage. Family members often feel emotionally and economically overwhelmed. They are discouraged and often feel powerless. Many value immediate gratification and do not want to "buy into" a long-term commitment. Some have long histories of unsatisfying relationships with social service, school, and law enforcement personnel. Other families are highly mobile and often have members living in various residences.

Troubled families can be particularly challenging to work with. Initial involvement in the intervention may be tenuous. Keeping such families connected to the long-term process can be frustrating. We have found the following techniques increase the likelihood of continued family participation:

- Families must be involved in the intervention quickly. Allow as little time as possible to lapse between acceptance into the intervention and the first meeting.
- Field consultants must be persistent and consistent in their efforts to engage these more challenging families. This may include frequent phone calls, notes on the front door, arriving unexpectedly, or when appropriate, meeting the client youth at school.
- Families must be held accountable for the active participation of all members. Field consultants must send a clear message that all members play an important role in the family and are expected to be involved in the process.
- Field consultants must be innovative and action oriented. Engagement occurs on an experiential basis rather than an intellectual one; interpersonal connection is made through active involvement. It follows that the particular interventions used should be relevant and enjoyable to the family. The initial activities used should be nonthreatening, fun, and meaningful. Moreover, the field consultants must communicate hope and the belief that the family's participation will have specific and tangible results.
- Field consultants and clinical staff must view assessment and intervention as an ongoing process. This view requires them to pay close attention to each family's level of involvement. It demands a flexible, creative, and dynamic orientation to helping families successfully move through each phase of the intervention.

THE FIELD CONSULTANTS

Role

The primary role of the field consultants, under clinical supervision, is to engage in inquiries, tasks, and activities designed to attain the goals and objectives of the FEI. To this end, the field consultants provide direction, constructive feedback, and information, and they establish a positive "work" atmosphere when meeting with families. Field consultants clarify the goals and objectives of the family and the intervention, review task and homework assignments, and facilitate family members' learning effective life skills. In addition, field consultants act as

- role models for good communication, healthy interpersonal boundaries, and leadership. On a more subtle level, field consultants model persistence of action, empathy, and optimism.
- referral sources for "system fits." For example, a field consultant may provide information regarding substance abuse counseling services or vocational training for a particular family member.
- liaisons between the client youth and other professionals/agencies in the community. When deemed appropriate, the field consultant facilitates linking the youth or family with an agency or community resource that can provide a specific service, such as job training or mentoring. Since the intervention's objective is family empowerment, primary responsibility for making these links is given to the client youth's caregivers, not the field consultant.

For legal and ethical reasons, it is critical that field consultants clarify the difference between *consultant* and *therapist* to families. Consultants do not provide psychological treatment services, which are beyond the scope of their educational and professional training. Nor do they perform clinical services that are provided by professionals licensed by the state. This clarification establishes realistic expectations for the family, as well as the competencies, and limitations, of the field consultant.

Qualifications

The field consultants in the YSP held bachelor-level degrees in the social sciences or education and had one to two years of experience working with high-risk youths. The success of the FEI primarily depends on the effectiveness of each field consultant. This effectiveness is based on several personal and professional competencies. As outlined below, YSP staff identified several competencies as critical to being a successful field consultant.

Self-Directedness

Being a field consultant requires a high degree of autonomy, self-organization, and focus. It is crucial that a field consultant be internally motivated rather than have a strong need for external structure. The degree of self-directedness is very much associated with the consultant's clear sense of the intervention's goals, vision, and philosophy. It is important that the consultant be effective in setting goals, implementing plans, and following through.

Ability to Tolerate Ambiguity

There are several reasons why it is important that the field consultant have a high tolerance for ambiguity. First, many of the families served are highly disorganized and chaotic, which results in unexpected and unpredictable situations at family meetings. Second, field consultants often work with families of different ethnic backgrounds, cultural values, and worldviews. These differences require the field consultants to suspend judgment and accept cultural and individual differences. Third, since the use of games, nonverbal exercises, and other symbolic activities is the cornerstone of the intervention, helping experiences often occur in a subtle, less-obvious manner. This lack of obvious change increases ambiguity and makes it difficult for the field consultant to see the shifts that are occurring. Finally, since many aspects of the helping process are intangible and difficult to measure, the field consultant must be able to continue his or her efforts with minimal feedback from participants. This lack of feedback can result in feelings of uncertainty and frustration if the field consultant is unable to tolerate a certain amount of ambiguity.

One of the many benefits of using videotapes in clinical supervision is that it offers visible and concrete feedback to the field consultant. This feedback lessens the degree of ambiguity the consultant experiences.

Nonjudgmental and Accepting

The capacity to respond meaningfully to a family in a caring and noncritical manner is essential. It is imperative that all families experience a high degree of positive regard by the field consultant; thus, an uncritical attitude must be present. This nonjudgmental position includes being emotionally supportive and nonblaming toward all who receive this intervention.

Communication Skills

The field consultant's training must include the development of effective communication skills. These skills are, primarily, active listening, paraphrasing, and the use of open-ended questions. Since the theoretical basis of this intervention is systemic, the field consultant must be able to communicate so as to increase meaningful interaction among family members. This circular style of interaction is designed to engage all members and facilitates positive communication within the family. Also, by emphasizing interaction among family members, the field consultant increases the members' sense of competency and their belief that they can operate in a constructive way.

Empathy

Empathy, the ability to see the world as another does, is a critical aspect of being an effective field consultant. The ability to suspend one's own world view so as to relate to the unique experiences of family members is vital to a successful intervention. This sensitivity is central to responding to family members in a caring and accepting manner.

Although empathy is a highly idiosyncratic trait, we have found that increasing empathy among field consultants is facilitated by

1. frequent and active involvement with families,
2. review of videotaped family visits with a supervisor,
3. the use of role-playing and other experiential activities in training and supervision, and
4. involvement in settings that are familiar to the family (i.e., scheduling a visit with the client youth at school, visiting the community's youth detention center).

An Orientation Toward Action

It is important that the field consultant take a highly active role in both the structure and process of the FEI. For example, a field consultant usually has to be persistent and tenacious in scheduling family meetings and setting an expectation that all members participate when appropriate. It is vital that the field consultant hold family members accountable for consistent participation in this intervention. Since successful participation in the FEI is based on families engaging in structured activities, moving through phases, and reaching specific goals, it is crucial that the field consultant provide initiative, direction, and leadership. Also, because many of the families involved with the juvenile justice system tend to think in concrete, rather than abstract, terms and are action oriented, as opposed to insight oriented, the field consultant will more powerfully engage members by the use of action-oriented approaches.

Self-Awareness

The role of field consultant requires insight, self-understanding, and self-reflection. The degree to which a field consultant genuinely understands himself or herself is very much related to his or her effectiveness with families. This understanding must include familial, social, and emotional forces that have affected his or her life. For example, one field consultant had a consistent pattern of avoiding family conflict by using humor to lessen his own discomfort. A clinical supervisor explored with him how earlier coping styles in his own family influenced his current behavior with families.

Along with self-awareness, it is important that field consultants develop the capacity for self-acceptance and have a commitment to personal growth. Like empathy, self-awareness is a highly idiosyncratic trait; however, certain environmental conditions enhance a field consultant's capacity for self-understanding. These conditions are

1. a trusting, emotionally safe relationship with the supervisory staff;
2. an overall atmosphere within the program of acceptance of, and support for, self-discovery; and
3. the program administration's sensitivity to, and respect for, the unique challenges of this form of field experience.

Initial Training of Field Consultants

Prior to implementing a family intervention, new field consultants undergo four to six weeks of training under the coaching and guidance of project clinical staff and more experienced field consultants. During this period they

1. receive instruction in the theoretical foundations of the FEI;
2. learn the policies and procedures involved, and the various activities used, in the intervention—as well as various community resources; and
3. shadow more experienced field consultants with active family caseloads.

When clinical staff believe the trainee is ready, he or she is assigned a family to work with. Here again, the field consultant receives coaching and guidance from a clinical supervisor. Videotapes of family meetings are a major tool for improving technique. As the field consultant's clinical supervisor gains confidence in the field consultant's ability to implement the intervention, the consultant's caseload is increased until a full caseload is reached. After the introductory and transition periods, field consultants are expected to handle six family cases simultaneously.

ROLES AND RESPONSIBILITIES OF KEY SUPERVISORY PERSONNEL

The key supervisory personnel for the YSP were the project director, clinical coordinator, and line clinical supervisors. Their major responsibilities are outlined below. Clinical directorship of the project changed in March 1996, but the conceptual foundation of the intervention and the roles of supervisory personnel and field consultants remained unchanged.

Project Director

Coordinate interface between project and service agencies and programs.
Allocate project resources.
Help maintain the integrity of the project's intervention and research activities.
Oversee and support all project staff.

Hire new staff and handle personnel matters.
Help orient and train clinical supervisors and field consultants.
Help enroll new youths and families into the project.

Clinical Coordinator

Help hire, orient, and train new field consultants.
Provide in-service training to field consultants.
Help provide group supervision to field consultants.
Help ensure the integrity of intervention services through the
supervision of line clinical supervisors.

Line Clinical Supervisors

Help hire, orient, and train new field consultants.
Provide in-service training to field consultants.
Provide weekly case supervision for field consultants.
Help provide group supervision to field consultants.
Serve as role models and mentors to field consultants.
Oversee the completion of field consultants' progress reports on
families.

CLINICAL POLICIES

The implementation of the FEI was guided by a number of clinical
policies. Those policies are discussed under three broad headings:
working with families, ensuring family and staff safety, and intervening in crisis situations. The policies were established for the FEI in
Tampa, Florida. They should be regarded as examples of policies that
can be established in other jurisdictions.

Working with Families

The following policies have been found to be critical to engaging
families and moving them through the intervention to graduation.
1. Any new family assigned to a field consultant should receive
an initial contact within twenty-four hours of referral. The first appointment for a meeting should be made within three working days, if
possible, but no longer than within five working days. This policy

will ensure that the first call and meeting take place within the "crisis period" for the family.

2. Families will be formally considered part of the FEI upon completion of their first family meeting.

3. Families are to be treated with respect at all times. No matter how challenging, family members are never to be shouted at, verbally abused, shoved or otherwise touched in an aggressive way, or subjected to any hostile/violent acts by a field consultant except in a very rare instance of necessary self-defense.

4. All family sessions are to be either videotaped (preferable) or audiotaped. Signatures are to be secured on the release form from all parties present at any meeting or visit. One signature from each person is sufficient, so that only new participants are to be asked to sign after the first session. The only exceptions to this policy are sessions that take place at the jail or other secure facility, instances in which families raise serious and adamant objections to being taped, and sites where the use of electricity is impossible (i.e., a walk with a client youth). In the latter cases, the field consultant will be expected to provide written documentation of the substantive content of the session immediately following its conclusion in lieu of a taped record.

5. Staff members are not to socialize with families in the project. They will meet with families at scheduled "work" sessions only. If invited to participate in a family event, such as a party or a shower, the staff member is to decline politely and clearly state that it would be "against the rules" to accept. If a gift is appropriate, a $10 gift certificate is to be purchased and given in the name of the project. Costs should be charged against the project's Sunshine Fund. No other exchange of gifts or social amenities is permitted, with the exception of inexpensive greeting cards that may be sent to mark special occasions.

6. Occasionally, supplies such as games and art materials are appropriately left with families to use as consumables. These materials are to be purchased by the project and clearly labeled as supplies for clinical activities toward completion of goals, not as gifts given by the field consultant.

7. No staff member is to accept any gift, tip, meal, or other favor from any family or family member. When food or drink is offered, the project representative is to decline politely, except under very rare

circumstances (e.g., a coughing fit or extreme heat) when a drink of water is needed.

8. Wherever possible, at the outset of each family meeting, the field consultant should attempt to have family members seated according to generational lines to establish and underscore family hierarchy and boundaries. If possible and appropriate, the field consultant should sit beside the client youth and act as advocate for the youth.

9. Ideally, each family is to have three meetings per week with the field consultant. Each meeting should last approximately one hour, but no longer than seventy-five minutes. If three meetings in a given week are not possible, telephone contact should be made to ensure three contacts per week.

10. If the client youth or a parent/guardian is incarcerated, meetings will be conducted at the incarceration site whenever possible. To the extent possible, activities toward completion of goals should continue. Meetings may be conducted with less frequency than listed in Policy 9, but as soon as release of the family member occurs, regular meetings should be resumed. Graduation may be provisionally delayed until release and all necessary criteria are met.

11. The FEI is a short-term, intensive intervention. Therefore, every effort should be made to complete the intervention within the ten to twelve week time frame listed in the original protocol. Because families differ greatly in the speed with which they meet goals, the intervention may last as few as five meetings (never fewer) and as many as forty-five, the maximum allowed without special approval by the field consultant's clinical supervisor and the clinical coordinator.

12. If a family cannot be located, has not returned telephone calls, or is in any other way unreachable, three attempts are to be made over a period of three weeks to reestablish contact and hold family meetings. If these efforts are unsuccessful, a letter is to be sent to the family inviting them to continue the intervention by responding within a two-week period. If this letter is unsuccessful, a letter will be sent (or, if necessary, a telephone call to someone in touch with the family) to indicate that they are (a) no longer active in the intervention, (b) invited to call the project office at any time to reinitiate FEI activities, and (c) to receive follow-up calls from the project staff. However, if the field consultant, in consultation with the clinical supervisor, be-

lieves that goals may still be met, a family may be placed in the graduation provisionally delayed/on-hold category.

13. When a family's status changes from active to closed or provisionally delayed/on hold, a change-of-status form is to be completed and signed by the field consultant and clinical supervisor and filed with copies of necessary letters for closure/status change.

14. No family is to be changed from active, ongoing service without the approval of the field consultant's supervisor.

15. Approval for status change to "graduated" is to be discussed with the field consultant's supervisor, based on fulfillment of the nine goals of the intervention (see "Goals" section), before a decision is made.

16. In cases in which the field consultant and supervisor disagree regarding readiness for graduation or any other change of status, the clinical coordinator will mediate until a resolution is reached.

17. Progress toward completion of goals will vary by family. However, every attempt is to be made to follow those outlined in the section "Phases of the FEI."

18. In rare instances (e.g., a field consultant leaves or scheduling problems occur), it may be necessary to transfer a family from one field consultant to another. The field consultant familiar with the family is responsible for providing a written summary statement and documentation stating the reason for the transfer. The supervisor of each field consultant is to approve the change. Whenever possible, both field consultants should make a transitional visit to the family together.

19. If a staff member is away (vacation, illness, personal leave, or the like), coverage is to be arranged. A clinical supervisor arranges coverage with another supervisor or the clinical coordinator. A field consultant arranges coverage with another field consultant, preferably one who is supervised by the same supervisor.

20. A family that requests reenrollment after having been closed, placed on hold, or in very rare instances, having graduated, will have that request considered by the clinical supervisors and clinical coordinator. If the decision is made to reenroll the family, the original field consultant will be assigned for any family moving from on hold status to active status. In all other cases, if reenrollment is approved, assignment will be made by the clinical supervisory staff.

Ensuring Family and Staff Safety

Since intervention services are provided in the field, considerable attention must be given to developing and maintaining procedures for ensuring the safety of all concerned. The following policies were established to ensure that field consultants take every reasonable precaution to protect the safety and security of family members and themselves.

1. Field consultants going into the field should sign out on a control board at the unit's office. Sign-out and projected return times should be monitored by supervisory staff and steps taken to contact staff who are in the field but not heard from for longer than reasonably expected periods of time. Field consultants should also carry beepers so that headquarters staff can page them for a check-in call. Further, field consultants should carry mobile phones and should be expected to maintain contact with project headquarters when they are in the field. Any requests from field consultants for information, support, or assistance should be responded to immediately.

2. All concerns about safety are to be discussed with the field consultant's supervisor as soon as possible, not only at supervisory sessions. If, for safety reasons, it is necessary to adjust the intervention, the clinical coordinator should also be consulted.

3. In situations that appear to involve safety concerns, field consultants should be accompanied by another staff member on visits to families. If a home environment is considered to be unsafe, arrangements should be made for family meetings to be held in a local neighborhood center, such as a church, day care center, or community service center.

4. Following the Tarasoff case in California, therapists having reason to believe a client is likely to harm another person are required to take steps to protect that other person from being hurt. Our field consultants are also expected to warn those who have been threatened. (In the Tarasoff case, a psychologist was held liable for monetary damages by the California Supreme Court because he failed to warn a potential victim his client threatened to kill, and then the client carried out his threat [*Tarasoff v. Regents of the University of California*, 1976].)

5. During the course of their work, field consultants may receive injuries or experience incidents involving clients or their families

(e.g., client threats). These injuries or experiences should be reported immediately, and the forms recording those events should be placed in the project files. Consistent with YSP policy, an injury report or incident report (or both if needed) must also be completed and submitted to the project director for review and follow-up action.

Crisis Intervention

Field consultants are trained to identify and respond quickly to family crises, particularly in the areas of alcohol or drug abuse, child abuse or neglect, and suicidal threats/behavior or other severe psychological conditions. Where possible, the highest-priority emergency response by community crisis teams should be established for all families enrolled in the intervention. The following are the crisis-intervention procedures established for the FEI.

1. Youths needing detoxification and stabilization services for alcohol and other substance abuse can be referred to the Agency for Community Treatment Services' (ACTS) Addiction Receiving Facility, located on the ground floor of the Juvenile Assessment Center building. This short-term program, which evaluates and refers youths needing additional services to specific agencies, is open twenty-four hours a day, seven days a week. A number of community substance abuse treatment programs also exist to treat adults.

2. By Florida law, professionals working with children are required to report cases of suspected child abuse or neglect to the Department of Child and Family Services and immediately inform his or her supervisor. The telephone number is 1-800-96-ABUSE. For parents/guardians who appear at risk of harming their children, the following resources are available to project staff: (a) Tampa's Child Abuse Council, telephone (813) 251-8080, and (b) two national help lines—1-800-FLA-LOVE (available twenty-four hours) and 1-800-FOR-A-CHILD. Parents are informed of these reporting requirements during the consent process.

3. Suicidal thoughts and behavior and other mental health problems also require quick and effective responses. For the FEI, arrangements were made with the Mobile Crisis Response Team, telephone (813) 272-2958, to provide crisis intervention and psychiatric services for client youths, siblings, and their parents/guardians. The crisis team is staffed by trained clinicians, who provide on-site mental

health evaluations. The FEI project has highest priority with the crisis team. When contacting the crisis team, the field consultant is to identify the project and explain the circumstances/priority to the extent possible.

ENSURING THE INTEGRITY
OF INTERVENTION SERVICES

It is essential that field consultants be adequately trained to implement and maintain high-quality intervention services. The maintenance of quality services within the FEI is an ongoing process that includes the following elements:

1. *Weekly meetings with clinical supervisors:* Field consultants meet with their clinical supervisor once a week for ninety minutes to review their families' cases and to obtain guidance on strategies and activities to use in helping families reach the intervention's goals.
2. *Biweekly group supervision meetings:* During these meetings, field consultants show videotapes of family meetings to the other field consultants and clinical staff and obtain ideas and coaching on how to work more effectively with family members.
3. *Weekly in-service training sessions:* Each week, field consultants receive ninety minutes of training on various topics relating to the intervention, for example, its theoretical foundations, the connection between specific goals of the intervention and activities used in working with families, new community agencies/services, and the procedures to use for "system fits."
4. *Biweekly clinical staff and project director meetings:* At these meetings, the project director and clinical staff (line clinical supervisors and clinical coordinator) discuss administrative issues affecting service delivery (e.g., coordination with other agencies supervising client youths) and issues affecting the integrity of service delivery (e.g., training topics); steps are taken to resolve these issues.
5. *Weekly project meetings:* Each week, field consultants, clinical staff, and administrative staff (i.e., the project director and administrative assistant/coordinator) meet to discuss any issues af-

fecting the delivery of quality services (e.g., caseload size), share information (e.g., new community services), review family enrollment into the intervention, and reaffirm commitment to the FEI goals.

Individual Clinical Supervision

The clinical supervisor-field consultant relationship is a critical factor in the effectiveness of intervention services. Since the intervention utilizes BA-level paraprofessionals, the need for a consistent, emotionally supportive supervisory relationship is an essential ingredient for success. Ninety-minute individual supervisory meetings are held weekly with each field consultant.

The role and function of the supervisor are multidimensional; the supervisor provides technical expertise, emotional support, administrative assistance, mentoring, and clinical training and education. We have identified a number of key elements of effective field consultant supervision.

1. Provide specific and concrete instruction to field consultants, including an emphasis on skill building in the areas of family systems theory, structural and strategic interventions, life skills (e.g., communication, conflict resolution, anger management), and interpersonal relations. The use of video- or audiotaped family meetings is an integral component of successful instruction.

2. Provide direction and encouragement to the field consultant about further training and educational opportunities (e.g., local workshops, relevant books and journals, university course work).

3. Teach and model effective clinical skills, including empathy, positive regard, and acceptance, as well as specific family systems techniques and interventions.

4. Instruct field consultants in the theory and use of the intervention's games and other activities.

5. Assist in decisions about phase determination for a particular family. To what degree is the family meeting its own, and the intervention's, goals? What impasses are the family members, client youth, or field consultant experiencing? What activities

or interventions might support positive change for the family? How can these changes most effectively be monitored?

6. Assist field consultants who are working through their own personal issues. As in any helping relationship, the caregiver's insight and self-awareness are key in maintaining healthy interpersonal boundaries, establishing clear goals, and conducting self-calibration. The supervisor is instrumental in facilitating increased self-understanding by the field consultant. The supervisory relationship offers a supportive atmosphere for field consultants to examine the impact of their own family system, gain greater sensitivity to cultural influences and assumptions, and develop a better understanding of, and for, their emotional world.

7. Provide emotional and professional support to field consultants. This support includes sharing clinical feedback, encouragement, and technical skills that increase a field consultant's level of expertise and confidence.

8. Be a "sounding board" for field consultants to facilitate their creative problem solving and innovative use of existing interventions and activities and to brainstorm ideas and strategies with which to foster positive change within a family.

9. Help organize the field consultants' daily and weekly activities.

10. Reinforce the intervention's goals, theoretical orientation, and vision.

Group Supervision

Group supervision meetings are held biweekly for two hours. These meetings comprise all field consultants, clinical supervisors, the clinical coordinator, and the project director. These meetings offer instruction and case supervision using the video- or audiotapes made by the field consultants during family meetings. Usually, each field consultant brings one or two tapes to be reviewed and discussed by all staff. The focus of discussion is primarily on the following:

- Feedback regarding family process, dynamics, and interaction
- Feedback on the responses and specific interventions of the field consultant

- Review of goals and objectives of the intervention as they relate to the particular family
- Development of clinical hypotheses and interventions

Along with training and education, group supervision offers an invaluable opportunity for providing professional support for field consultants. The group supervisory process provides a supportive environment in which to share ideas and feelings, examine specific challenges, and increase self-understanding. In doing so, the work of all staff improves and relationships become strengthened. The benefits of group supervision also include:

1. receiving peer support and technical assistance,
2. strengthening a sense of bondedness and professional support,
3. developing a shared connection, thereby decreasing professional isolation, and
4. acquiring understanding and skills through vicarious learning.

In-Service Training

Ongoing training for field consultants is another critical aspect of the FEI. Training is provided for ninety minutes a week by one of the clinical staff. In general, all training has a strong experiential component, which enhances both the conceptual and practical dimensions of the learning experience. In addition, field consultants have many opportunities for training off-site and for attending in-service programs given by other professionals in the community. It is critical, however, that continual linkage be maintained between these activities and exercises and the goals of the intervention so that the integrity of the intervention is maintained.

There are three major content areas in the in-service training:

1. *Use and refinement of family activities:* Although it is important for field consultants to have a theoretical understanding of the family activities used in the intervention, great emphasis is placed on "hands-on" experience. The benefits of this experiential approach are twofold: field consultants

   - learn how to use these innovative approaches effectively through behavioral rehearsal and
   - increase their empathy for the families with whom they work.

Furthermore, these sessions provide opportunities to role-play specific challenges presented by a particular family. This training is an excellent vehicle for sharing constructive feedback; modifying, updating, and fine-tuning materials; and developing new materials for families.

2. *General topics in the helping process:* The YSP provided training on a wide range of topics, including systems theory, structural and strategic interventions, family and human development, and life management skills. Examples of some areas of concentration are:

- Systems Theory: Information on family organization, boundaries, hierarchies, communications processes, alliances, and power issues; the impact of the wider culture on the family; the family as a dynamic system that affects, and is affected by, its members; the clinical use and meaning of the genogram.
- Family and Human Development: Individual and family development from a life-cycle perspective; normative psychosocial developmental tasks of childhood, adolescence, and adulthood; gender and ethnicity within the family context.
- Life Management: Effective communication skills for all family members; the development of conflict-resolution, negotiation, and anger-management strategies; goal-setting, problem-solving, and time-management skills.

3. *The unique issues affecting "at-risk" youths:* Issues in addiction; at-risk, resiliency, and cultural diversity issues for children and teens; depression and suicide; violence prevention; sexuality and teen pregnancy; the juvenile justice system; community resources and referrals.

IMPLEMENTING THE FEI

The YSP provided an exciting opportunity to use the FEI to intervene effectively in the lives of juvenile offenders and their families. This intervention sought to strengthen the most significant determinant of favorable long-term outcomes for children: improving the family's functioning and ability to find effective solutions for its problems. By intervening in the family system, the project's field consultants attempted to change the family's interactions in more healthful and appropriate directions. These changes in family functioning were expected to result in more prosocial changes in the client youth's behavior. The short- and long-term impact of the intervention on the client youths' delinquent/criminal behavior, alcohol and other drug use, and emotional/psychological functioning is evaluated in Chapters 4, 5, and 6, respectively.

Chapter 3

Youths and Families Involved in the Youth Support Project

The Youth Support Project (YSP) was based at the Hillsborough County Juvenile Assessment Center (JAC), located in Tampa, Florida. Established in 1993, the JAC is a centralized intake facility where youths taken into custody on delinquency charges are brought for processing. The JAC also has a separate intake and processing component for truant youths. The truancy programs of the Tampa Police Department and the Hillsborough County Sheriff's Department began operations on January 4, 1993; the delinquency component was implemented in May 1993.

SETTING FOR THE YSP

The JAC is an outgrowth of several years of planning and preparation in Hillsborough County, and it reflects a growing appreciation that the crises in the county's juvenile justice systems necessitate collaborative, interagency efforts (Dembo and Brown, 1994). The JAC provides an important opportunity to involve troubled youths in helping services and intervention programs before they become deeply involved in the juvenile justice system. Colocated at the facility are law enforcement juvenile booking functions, delinquency intake functions of the Florida Department of Juvenile Justice (DJJ), community mental health services, the status offender intake program of the Hillsborough County Department of Children's Services, and truancy program staff from the Hillsborough County School Board, the

Hillsborough County Sheriff's Office, and the Tampa Police Department. The easy availability of these agencies enabled us to

1. complete preliminary screening of processed youths to identify potential problems requiring referrals for in-depth assessments,
2. complete in-depth psychosocial assessments of referred youths,
3. ensure that youths' service needs are addressed in dispositional recommendations,
4. link at-risk or troubled youths and their families with needed services,
5. track the outcomes of the problem-identification and program-linking activities.

The JAC facility helps overcome major workload and "systemic" juvenile justice problems in responding to troubled youths. The Tampa facility is coordinated by a community service agency (ACTS, Inc.) and staffed with clinicians. The facility is located above and supported by the presence of ACTS' twenty-bed, twenty-four-hour-a-day adolescent detoxification and stabilization program; this unit has around-the-clock nursing staff and medical, psychological, and psychiatric back-up services.

The JAC has a comprehensive information system consisting of three parts: (1) preliminary screening data, (2) in-depth assessment data, and (3) referral and referral outcome data. Each processed youth is given a unique identification number and, for each entry, a unique event/episode number. The information system is event or episode based, which permits analyses by individual case or by event/episode.

The comprehensive information system includes the following information: demographic characteristics (e.g., gender, age, race/ethnicity, socioeconomic status [SES]); current charges; delinquency history; dependency history (e.g., physical abuse, sexual abuse, neglect); special case designation (Missing Children Community Action Program [M-CAP] case, Serious Habitual Offender Community Action Program [SHOCAP] case, gang associate case); DJJ service/program history; educational history (current grade, standardized test results, and special program placement [e.g., emotionally handicapped, specific learning disability]; self-reported alcohol and other drug use (prevalence, recency, lifetime frequency, and past year days of use of alcohol, marijuana/hashish, inhalants, hallucinogens, powdered or liquid cocaine, crack, heroin, and the nonmedical use of sedatives, tranquilizers, stimulants, and analgesics); urine test results for cannabinoids, cocaine, barbiturates, amphetamines, opiates, and PCP; HIV-risk behavior (injection drug use, needle/works sharing); substance abuse and mental health treatment history; and dispositional, assessment, and immediate placement recommendations.

Indication of each youth's potential problems in one or more of ten psychosocial functioning areas was obtained by use of the Problem Oriented Screening Instrument for Teenagers (POSIT; Rahdert, 1991): substance use/abuse, physical health status, mental health status, family relationships, peer relations, educational status, vocational status, social skills, leisure and recreation, and aggressive behavior and delinquency. The POSIT is designed to identify whether a problem requiring further assessment and perhaps treatment may exist in any functional area. Cutoff scores, and red-flag items in some instances, have been established for each functional area to indicate the need for further assessment.

Information included in the preliminary screening package is secured from a number of agencies, including DJJ (for information on juvenile court appearances/action on delinquency charges and protective services information on abuse and neglect issues), the Tampa Police Department, the Hillsborough County Sheriff's Department, and the Hillsborough County School System. The ACTS staff who collect the preliminary screening data are trained in rapport building, interviewing skills, and the use of the instruments themselves. This training facilitates the collection of reliable and valid data from the youths.

SELECTING YOUTHS AND FAMILIES FOR ENROLLMENT IN THE YSP

Youths processed at the JAC (Dembo and Brown, 1994) who were arrested on misdemeanor or felony charges were sampled for inclusion in the project. When openings occurred on the field consultants' caseloads, a list of recently arrested youths processed at the JAC was drawn. These cases were classified by gender and a variable reflecting race/ethnicity: Hispanic (Latino), black non-Hispanic (African

American), and white non-Hispanic (Anglo). Equal numbers of youths in each of these six cells were randomly selected, and their parents/ guardians were approached regarding enrollment in the project. Over-sampling of females and Hispanic youths was designed to improve statistical power for gender and race/ethnicity comparisons. Although this oversampling prevents the use of the data collected to generalize to the population of youths processed at the JAC, that was not the major purpose of the project. This procedure and the large sample size pro-vided good representation of African-American, Latino, and Anglo youths of both sexes and their families, and they improved statistical power for group comparisons.

Following initial screening of the youths, we excluded youths and families from enrollment in the project for a number of nonclinical reasons. As Table 3.1 shows, of the 1,582 families we initially screened for involvement in the project, 820 (52 percent) were excluded. The majority of excluded cases involved families of youths who lived out-side Hillsborough County (i.e., the youths were arrested in Hills-borough County but lived outside the county) or outside the project service radius of thirty miles of Tampa, and youths picked up on an

TABLE 3.1. Enrollment History of YSP Families (Families Screened/Contacted, n = 1,582, September 1, 1994 - January 31, 1998)

Excluded	n = 820	(52%)	Not Excluded	n = 762	(48%)
Reasons for Exclusion	(n = 820)		*Result*	(n = 762)	
Lives outside Hillsborough County or service radius of pro-ject (within thirty miles of Tampa); family leaving town for an extended period of time; or family moved out of county be-fore enrollment completed.	332	40%	Consented	322	42%
			Refused	228	30%
			Case closed	212	28%
			Reasons for Closing Case	(n = 212)	
Picked up on a warrant (not a new arrest)	198	24%	Family does not respond to project	78	37%
Family cannot read or speak English	51	6%	Unable to contact or locate family	61	29%
Youth living on own/no family	50	6%	Family cancels/fails to show for in-depth assessment	19	9%
Family already in project	45	5%			
Youth facing long-term incarcer-ation/placement	44	5%	Family already receiving similar services	15	7%
Youth is an adult	36	4%	Youth ran away	11	5%
Youth under eleven years of age	20	2%	Other reasons	28	13%
Other reasons	44	5%			

outstanding warrant for failure to appear in court on a previous arrest charge.

Seven hundred and sixty-two youths (48 percent) were not excluded from screening/enrollment into the project. Parents or guardians of youths in nonexcluded families were contacted by telephone or home visit (if no telephone was available) to determine their interest in taking part in the project. Our initial contact involved describing the project, informing family members that their participation was voluntary, reviewing our data collection activities, and summarizing the services the families would be assigned to receive—Family Empowerment Intervention (FEI) or Extended Services Intervention (ESI). We answered any questions the parents or guardians had; if they were interested in learning more about the project, we scheduled an initial interview to complete baseline data collection.

Of the 762 families, 322 families (42 percent) agreed to enroll, 315 of whom had become involved in the project by January 31, 1998. This was the cutoff date for youths and families involved in the YSP for whom we would complete the various outcome analyses to examine the impact of the FEI. This decision was based on the need to have a follow-up period of sufficient length to examine the short- and long-term effects of the FEI. The YSP continued to enroll families through September 30, 1998; 394 families were ultimately served by the project. However, this study focuses on the 315 families enrolled through January 31, 1998.

Thirty percent of the 762 nonexcluded families refused to participate in the project. The other 28 percent of the nonexcluded families had their cases closed for a number of reasons. The majority of closed cases involved families that failed to respond to attempts to contact them or who could not be contacted by project staff. Many of the families we were unable to locate or contact involved youths who gave incorrect family addresses and telephone numbers when processed at the JAC. The information presented in Table 3.1 provides a vivid indication of the challenges of getting families with youths entering the juvenile justice system to participate in voluntary service programs. Figure 3.1 provides a flowchart of family enrollment in the YSP, a process discussed in more detail in the following text.

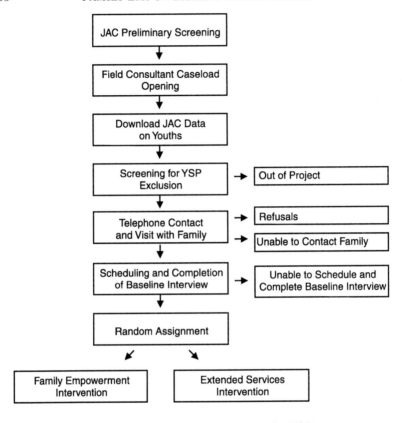

FIGURE 3.1. Flow of Families into the YSP

Gender and Race/Ethnicity Representation in the YSP

As Table 3.2 shows, gender, racial, and ethnic diversity were achieved in the project. Although we intended to have approximately equal numbers in the six cells shown in the table, there were substantially fewer in the Hispanic female cell than in the five other cells. This may be due partly to the relative rarity of Hispanic females in the JAC population, so that an Hispanic female was not always available for selection. The effect of our selection procedures was to over-sample females (who normally comprise 25 percent of the youths processed at the JAC), oversample Hispanic youths, and undersample African-American youths.

TABLE 3.2. Gender and Race/Ethnicity Representation in the YSP

Race/Ethnicity	Females	Males	Total	Percent (n = 315)
Hispanic	25	53	78	25%
African American	59	60	119	38%
Anglo or other*	58	60	118	37%
Total	142	173	315	100%
Percent of total	45%	55%		

*Native American, Asian American, and mixed ethnicity

Early Study of Enrollment

In an early study of enrollment in the YSP, we examined the enrollment outcomes of the first 385 families selected for potential involvement in the project (Dembo, Cervenka, et al., 1999). Overall, 34 percent of the families were excluded from the project for the reasons presented in Table 3.1. As in the entire sample, the most frequent reason for exclusion was that the family was living outside, or about to move outside, Hillsborough County or the thirty-mile service radius of the project (40 percent). Of the families that were not excluded, 48 percent consented to complete the enrollment process and participate in the project, 32 percent refused, and 19 percent were "closed." Most of the closed cases involved families we were unable to locate despite repeated efforts or families that did not respond to our attempts to contact them.

The families that were excluded or nonexcluded were compared on eighteen demographic and psychosocial variables. Only two statistically significant differences were found between the two groups: (1) youths living in mother-only households were less likely to be included in the project, and (2) youths arrested on felony charges were more likely to be included in the project. A second comparison distinguished between families that consented or refused. The only significant factor distinguishing these two types of families was that families of older-aged youths were less likely to consent to participate than families of younger-aged youths.

Guiding Principles of Enrollment in the YSP

Several guiding principles informed our enrollment activities. First, *successful enrollment requires both qualitative and quantitative monitoring.* Project research staff, who enrolled families in the YSP and completed the in-depth baseline and follow-up interviews, received training on the nature, purposes, and activities of the FEI and ESI. They had a working understanding of the FEI. This knowledge prepared them to answer effectively any questions interested families had about the project. Research staff also shared strategies for contacting families. In addition, they routinely reviewed individual experiences regarding enrollment successes and failures so that enrollment techniques that failed could be eliminated. Successful enrollment strategies were used to enhance enrollment procedures. Enrollment challenges and successful strategies were also shared during weekly project meetings, which were attended by all YSP staff. We constantly sought to increase our success rate by identifying strong and weak aspects of enrollment.

Quantitative information is also essential for effective enrollment. A project-developed database enabled us to prepare weekly updates on the enrollment process. These data were especially useful in anticipating when new cases had to be selected and in tracking families as they moved through the various stages of the FEI process.

Second, as discussed in Chapter 2, *engaging,* the interpersonal process whereby a field consultant connected with the family in an empathetic and positive manner, was routinely used to increase the family's acceptance of the field consultant and its active involvement in the project. Project research staff also sought to engage with families during the enrollment process in an effort to increase positive feelings about the YSP and to improve the likelihood that they would feel the project was a serious, caring program of services in which they wanted to participate. Engaging also represented a beginning step in establishing respect and trust, which would be followed throughout the YSP.

The third guiding principle is *timing.* It is much easier to break through family resistance to change when a family is in crisis than when the family is experiencing complacency. Families in crisis experience an upset in the family system and they are often anxious to regain system balance once again. In the YSP, we referred to this circumstance as a "window of opportunity," whereby we quickly stepped in during the crisis created by the child's arrest to enroll the family in the project. We were aware that the arrested youth is often crying out for help, the parents/guardians are concerned for their child's well-being, and the family can benefit from either the Family Empowerment or Extended Services intervention. The YSP staff were committed to contributing to the families' well-being and believed that both interventions were valuable.

Experiences Enrolling Families in the YSP

We learned to regard successful enrollment in the project as a multicontact process. Often, four or more contacts with the parents/guardians were required before the family began the FEI or ESI (Dembo, Cervenka, et al., 1999). First, we had an initial contact with the family (usually by telephone) to explain both intervention services and random assignment and to schedule an in-depth baseline interview. Second, we obtained the family's formal consent to participate and collected in-depth data from the youth and parents/guardian; third, we telephoned to inform the family what its intervention assignment was and what would be expected of them. If a family was assigned to the FEI group, we informed them that a field consultant would be contacting them shortly. Fourth, a letter was sent to the family that described our staff's commitment with regard to their assigned intervention. The four examples that follow illustrate how we approached the enrollment of families on an individual basis.

Family 1

Family 1 presented some unique challenges to enrollment in the Youth Support Project. The family consisted of a single, unemployed mother, who cared for her eleven-year-old daughter (client youth), two sons, and disabled mother. Several phone calls were made before actually speaking with Ms. R. Initially, Ms. R was very suspicious of any agency associated with the juvenile justice system. The phone conversation focused on informing Ms. R what the project consisted of, answering questions, and attending to all of her concerns. Ms. R needed a great deal of reassurance and seemed very surprised that someone would listen to her concerns and offer services to assist her family. She stated that several agencies she worked with in the past had not kept their promises about the services they offered. She felt that they did not listen to her and treated her like a case number. After a lengthy discussion, Ms. R agreed to a home appointment to discuss further what the YSP offered.

During the home visit, the research associate suggested to Ms. R that her daughter be taken to the YSP office for assessment since the house was very small and she could not move her disabled mother. Ms. R became very suspicious and thought the YSP might be trying to put her daughter back in detention. She no longer wanted to participate in the YSP. At this point, it was clear that Ms. R needed to see all the information about the YSP and have the services explained in greater detail. The research associate asked Ms. R if she would let him go through all the YSP materials and stressed that he would find a way to do her daughter's assessment in the home. He assured her that the project was voluntary, not part of the court system, and not designed to be punitive. At several points, Ms. R tested what the research associate told her and expressed her fears. Finally, Ms. R's trust was won, and he proceeded with the in-depth interview.

This case illustrates how families carry over their prior experience with other service agencies. Ms. R felt she had been mistreated by other agencies and so her enrollment was focused on addressing those issues. She was treated with respect and given time to discuss her concerns and frustrations. These efforts were critical in bridging the gap that had formed between Ms. R's family and community services.

Family 2

Family 2 consisted of a single mother, her three adolescent sons, and two of her best friend's children. Several contacts were made before establishing an interview date. The mother was in severe crisis over two of her sons running away, threatening her with violence, and being arrested for various violations. She was afraid and felt she had lost control of her family and that no one could or would assist her. Time was spent on the phone listening to her concerns about her family and letting her know how the YSP would commit to working with her family members and supporting them with one of the interventions. The mother was skeptical, but stated that she would try since she felt she could no longer handle her sons alone.

Flexibility and patience were essential with this family since the circumstances were very stressful and intense. The client youth had to be interviewed in the detention center while the mother was interviewed in the home. The youth was very reluctant at first, but after speaking with YSP staff and his mother he agreed to participate. The mother had to cancel once due to her work schedule and was resistant to rescheduling. Phone contacts were continued on a regular basis and the mother eventually consented to another interview time.

During her interview the mother was very anxious and afraid for her family. She was a strong and independent woman who supported all five children with her one job. She was very proud that she was not on public assistance and felt ashamed that she had to turn to someone to help her with her children. Her second son ran away an hour before the interview and was arrested for shoplifting. The police called during our interview to let her know he was arrested, and the mother cried and stated that she was glad that the YSP was going to help her.

This family's enrollment points out that during a major crisis parents are often hesitant to accept any kind of assistance but are also desirous of a change. Support, empathy, and commitment to work with a family are critical. Families such as this one present unique challenges that at first can be frustrating and may deter a community agency from working with them. The YSP enrollment process is designed to meet these challenges. Enrollment breaks through barriers put up by families and gives them a realistic chance at receiving services. But most important, families are heard, supported, and given the flexibility that families in crisis must have. The dynamics of these families must be understood and respected in order to be successful.

Family 3

Family 3 consisted of a single mother, Ms. A, and her three adolescent male children: the client youth (José), age sixteen, and his two younger brothers. Following several telephone calls, contact was made with the mother and an in-depth interview was scheduled.

Upon arrival at the household, which was located in a housing complex, the YSP staff member met with Ms. A, José, and one younger brother, age eleven. After asking several questions about the process of enrolling in the YSP and the various services that are provided by the project, Ms. A and the younger son seemed very interested in participating. Ms. A was particularly interested in obtaining training in word processing and in improving her ability to speak English. José, however, was guarded and showed little enthusiasm for the YSP. He indicated that his arrest on a shoplifting charge was an isolated, nonserious event and that he didn't have any problems.

In the ensuing conversation with José, the staff member pointed out that, even if he didn't have any problems, the YSP could help him and his family become what they wanted to become and assist him in obtaining a part-time job and locating training in video recording. José voiced concern about the amount of time that would be involved if he participated in the project, especially if his family was assigned to receive the FEI, which involved working with a field consultant for three hourly meetings a week for approximately ten weeks. In response to this concern, the YSP staff member asked José to consider how worthwhile it would be for him to invest thirty hours in the intervention phase of the project for the purpose of improving his life and future. The staff member stressed the importance of his being actively involved in the project if it was to have a beneficial effect. The conversation opened the possibility for a mutually collaborative effort. After some silence, the YSP staff member ended the meeting with a request that José consider again the opportunities the YSP would provide for him and his family, and he indicated he would call the family in a few days.

Two days after the home visit, the YSP staff member called the family and spoke with Ms. A. She indicated that her son had decided to participate in the YSP. An in-depth interview was scheduled for the next day. The following day, José telephoned the YSP staff member, said his mother was not feeling well, and requested that the in-depth interview be rescheduled for the following week. On the scheduled interview date, the YSP staff member visited the household and completed the in-depth interviews with Ms. A and José.

Several factors were important in the successful enrollment of this family in the YSP. Multiple contacts took place with the family, reflecting our continued interest and support in working with them. The family was treated with respect throughout the enrollment process. Further, and perhaps most critical for this family, the client youth was empowered with the decision for his enrollment in the project. Rather than repeating experiences he had with other institutions and agencies, which often told him what to do (e.g., the courts, school), we gave the client youth the choice about what he wanted to do with this opportunity to improve his life.

Family 4

In Family 4, the mother of the client youth was living in the home of her brother, to whom she paid rent. This arrangement was to last for four more months, at which time Ms. T planned to move to a nearby city. The client youth was a young adolescent female who had recently been placed in a juvenile detention center for retail theft and resisting arrest. Ms. T had gone through a ten-year, bitter divorce battle with her former husband, during which period the client youth had run away from her father's house for over a year.

When contacted by telephone, Ms. T agreed to participate in the YSP, although the YSP staff member scheduling the in-depth assessment with Ms. T indicated Ms. T had some concerns. Principal among these were her plans to move to a nearby city in a few months and her previous experience with helping agencies that failed to follow through on their promises. A YSP staff member met Ms. T at her brother's home as scheduled. Ms. T's concern about how her moving would affect her participation in the YSP were put to rest. She was advised that if she and her daughter were assigned to receive the Family Empowerment Intervention, this phase would be completed before their relocation. Ms. T was further informed that the city to which she planned to move was sufficiently close to Tampa for us to continue working together.

Ms. T's second concern was the most challenging. Ms. T claimed she had been referred by a state agency to a psychologist, who among other things, had promised to obtain a transfer for her daughter to attend a high school where she could meet more prosocial friends. Ms. T indicated the psychologist completed all the necessary paperwork and told her that a favorable decision would be forthcoming in a short time. Ms. T said nothing happened with this request, although the psychologist repeatedly claimed official notification would be received soon. Ms. T wondered whether the YSP would also fall short in its promise to provide assistance and support to her and her daughter. She urged that YSP staff not make any promises they were not prepared to deliver on. The YSP staff member spent over an hour addressing this issue with Ms. T. Acknowledging Ms. T's feelings of past disappointment, he reviewed the numerous ways in which YSP works with families and sought to assure her that promises would be kept.

Ms. T was working at a low-paying job and wanted to receive training to improve her typing skills so she could qualify for a better-paying position. She also asked the YSP staff member to find out how her daughter could be transferred to another high school. (Such a system-fit or service-linkage step would be appropriate for either of the interventions to which she could be assigned.) After completing Ms. T's in-depth interview, the YSP staff member returned to the project office to act quickly on Ms. T's requests. She was called within two days with concrete information and recommendations.

Four days after Ms. T's interview, the YSP staff member completed an in-depth interview with the client youth at the detention center. During the interview, the youth expressed a wish to transfer to another high school, and she was informed of the various contacts the YSP had made on her behalf in this regard and of what had been learned. This response impressed the client youth, as did the YSP staff member's indication that the YSP would assist her in her efforts to get a part-time job. She was informed that the YSP would begin to work with her and her mother as soon as she was released from the detention center.

Family 4 reflects a common experience. Many government health, social service, and juvenile justice agencies are overburdened and underfinanced. Workers are commonly assigned large caseloads of clients, and they spend much of their time dealing with crises and paperwork rather than providing support and intervention services. Requests for assistance often go unanswered for weeks, during which time stress and behavioral problems among family members increase. Many families feel "let down" by the "system" and are cynical about agency representatives' claims to be working with them. Helping them to break through their cynicism and facilitating their participation in their own improvement require persistence and keeping one's word.

DATA-COLLECTION PROCEDURES

Baseline Data Collection

In-depth baseline interviews were completed with 315 youths processed at the Hillsborough County JAC from September 1, 1994, through January 31, 1998. Each youth was paid $10 for completing this initial interview prior to being randomly assigned to the FEI or ESI. These interviews took one and one-half to two hours. Most of these interviews took place at the youths' homes or elsewhere in the community, although several interviews were completed at the local juvenile detention center where youths were temporarily held on their arrest charges.

The baseline interview included questions about demographics, education, mental health and substance abuse treatment history, family problems, friends' problem behavior, sexual victimization and physical abuse experiences, alcohol and illicit-drug use, delinquent behavior, and psychological functioning. Information was obtained from official records on youths' arrest charges at entering the JAC and their delinquency and dependency referral histories. Voluntary hair samples were collected and tested for use of five drugs (marijuana, cocaine, opiates, methamphetamines, and PCP) over the previous ninety days.

Follow-Up Data Collection

Depending on the year youths entered the project, we completed up to three annual follow-up interviews with each youth. Table 3.3 presents this information, together with our follow-up interview success rates.

As can be seen, overall reinterview rates of 86, 85, and 76 percent were achieved for the Time 1, Time 2, and Time 3 interviews, respectively. The follow-up interviews averaged one and one-half hours, and each youth was paid $20 for a completed follow-up interview. Importantly, we had a low refusal rate for each follow-up interview. Excluding youths who moved out of state (who were not routinely followed-up) and youths who could not be located, we achieved net reinterview rates of 94, 93, and 91 percent for the Time 1, Time 2, and Time 3 in-

TABLE 3.3. Follow-Up Interview Results Among Eligible Youths

Period of Baseline Interview	n	Follow-Up Interviews Sought
September 1, 1994 - January 31, 1996	120	Time 1, Time 2, Time 3
February 1, 1996 - January 31, 1997	80	Time 1, Time 2
February 1, 1997 - January 31, 1998	115	Time 1
Total	**315**	

Results/Status	Time 1 (n = 315)	Time 2 (n = 200)	Time 3 (n = 120)
Completed	86.3%	85.0%	75.8%
Lost Case	5.1%	6.0%	10.0%
Living out of State	2.5%	3.0%	6.7%
Refused	6.0%	6.0%	7.5%
Total	**99.9%**	**100%**	**100%**

terviews, respectively. There were no significant differences in the reinterview results for FEI and ESI youths. In addition, 94 percent of the Time 1 interviews, 93 percent of the Time 2 interviews, and 97 percent of the Time 3 interviews were completed within 120 days following the anniversary of the preceding interview.

The in-depth follow-up interview included questions about the youth's current living circumstances, as well as each of the topic areas covered in the baseline interview, with appropriate adjustments in time coverage for the relevant follow-up period. In addition, voluntary hair samples and urine specimens were collected for youths not incarcerated for longer periods than the surveillance window of each respective test (two days for the urine tests and ninety days for the hair tests). The urine specimens were tested for the presence of the same five drugs as the hair tests.

The follow-up interviews took place in a variety of settings at each interview wave. A majority of youths were interviewed at home or in another community location. However, other youths were interviewed in DJJ residential commitment programs, county jails, juvenile detention centers, prison, or another type of secure program. We used a variety of strategies to locate youths for reinterview. These strategies are presented in schematic form in Table 3.4.

TABLE 3.4. YSP Tracking Methods

---

1. If a telephone is listed for the family:

   1.1. Check Juvenile Assessment Center Registration Log for JAC entry since baseline (or last) interview. If registration information exists, record most recent contact information (address, telephone number, etc.).

   1.2. Check Youth Support Project family records for most recent contact information.

   1.3. If telephone is disconnected:

   1.3.1. Dial 411 for telephone information on client youth and family members

   1.3.2. Make a home visit:

   —If client youth no longer lives there, learn his/her whereabouts if possible. If family no longer lives at address, try to find as much location information as possible from current residents or neighbors (e.g., when moved, where family, youth may have gone).

2. If there is no telephone listed for the family:

   2.1. Review previous interview files, especially the most recent, and call relatives, friends, or 411 to see if there is a new telephone number.

   2.2. If 2.1 is unsuccessful, attempt to find updated address from the following information systems:

   —JAC

   —Florida Department of Juvenile Justice

   —Florida Department of Children and Families

   —Florida Department of Corrections

   —Hillsborough County School Board

   —State's Attorney's Office

   —Hillsborough County jail.

3. If Steps 1 and 2 are unsuccessful:

   3.1. Send identifying information on client youth and family (e.g., date of birth [DOB] and Social Security No. of youth, name and DOB of closest relative or guardian) to Florida Department of Motor Vehicles for clearance.

   3.2. If client youth is aged sixteen or over, a record clearance by the Florida Department of Labor can also be requested.

CHARACTERISTICS OF YOUTHS
AT BASELINE INTERVIEW

Demographic, Educational, and Treatment History

As shown in Table 3.2, the study consisted of youths who mostly were male (55 percent). Hispanic, African-American, and Anglo youths, respectively, comprised 25, 38, and 37 percent of the study group. The youths averaged 14.6 years of age (standard deviation = 1.60). Seventeen percent reported they lived with both biological parents, 50 percent with their mother only, and 14 percent with their mother and another adult. Most families had low to moderate socioeconomic status (based on 235 youths on whom we had information on the occupation of the household's chief wage earner or other sources of household income [derived from Fishburne, Abelson, and Cisin, 1980]). Fourteen percent of the chief wage earners held an executive, administrative/managerial, or professional/specialty type position; 17 percent held technical, sales, or administrative support positions; 6 percent held skilled positions; 50 percent held unskilled, semiskilled, or low/moderate skilled service positions; and 12 percent of the youths' households were supported by public funds.

Although most of the youths (87 percent) were still attending school, many had educational problems. For example, 42 percent reported being placed in a special educational program (e.g., emotionally handicapped, severe learning disorder) and 50 percent had repeated a grade in school. Most youths lagged one (42 percent) or two (16 percent) grade levels behind the grade that would be expected based on their chronological age.

Relatively few youths reported ever receiving mental health or substance abuse treatment. Sixteen percent reported receiving mental health care in the past, and 4 percent indicated they were currently being treated. Only 6 percent of the youths indicated they ever received treatment for a substance abuse problem, and 1 percent reported they were receiving care for alcohol or other drug problems at the time of their baseline interview.

Arrest Charges upon Entering the JAC

Almost all youths entered the JAC as a result of being taken into custody on one or more felony or misdemeanor charges. Half of the youths (fifty-two) had felony property charges (especially burglary, grand larceny, and auto theft). Misdemeanor property charges (e.g., retail theft) ranked second (41 percent). Sixteen percent of the youths were brought to the JAC on violent felony charges (e.g., robbery). Few youths were arrested on drug felony (6 percent) or misdemeanor (5 percent) charges, or on public disorder misdemeanor (9 percent) or violent misdemeanor (1 percent) charges.

Delinquency and Dependency Referral History

Information obtained from the DJJ indicated that 55 percent of the youths had been referred to the juvenile court at least once. Of those, 25 percent had been referred to juvenile court at least once for property felony offenses (e.g., burglary), 35 percent for misdemeanor property offenses (e.g., retail theft), 22 percent for misdemeanor violence offenses (e.g., assault), 18 percent for felony violence (e.g., robbery), and 17 percent for misdemeanor public disorder offenses (e.g., trespassing). Again, few youths had arrest records for felony drug (5 percent) or misdemeanor drug (6 percent) offenses.

The youths were victims as well as offenders. Seventeen percent had been referred to the Florida Department of Health and Rehabilitative Services for being physically abused, 16 percent for being neglected, and 7 percent for sexual abuse or exploitation.

Family Problems

As we discussed in Chapter 1, many juveniles entering the juvenile justice system are experiencing multiple problems in the areas of physical abuse, sexual victimization, poor emotional/psychological functioning, poor educational functioning, and alcohol and other drug use. In addition, they often live in families whose members have experienced problems with alcohol/other drug use, mental health, or crime. Many youths in the project came from families with psychosocial functioning difficulties. Youths reported that family or household family members had an alcohol abuse problem (35 percent); another drug abuse problem (24 percent; most frequently marijuana/ hashish); or an emotional or mental health problem (23 percent). In addition, members of the youths' families or household families often had had experience with the juvenile or adult justice system. Youths reported that a family or household family member had been arrested (65 percent); held in jail/detention (56 percent); adjudicated delinquent or convicted of a crime (45 percent); put on community control or probation (44 percent); or sent to a training school or prison (33 percent).

Physical Abuse

Drawing upon the work of Straus and his associates (Straus, 1979, 1983; Straus, Gelles, and Steinmetz, 1980), we used six items designed to determine the youths' physical abuse experiences. The youths were asked whether they had ever been beaten or *really* hurt by being hit, but not with anything (24 percent); been beaten or hit with a whip, strap, or belt (37 percent); been beaten or hit with something "hard," like a club or stick (15 percent); been shot with a gun, injured with a knife, or had some other "weapon" used against them (6 percent); been hurt badly enough to require (need) a doctor, bandages, or other medical treatment (10 percent); or spent time in a hospital because they were physically injured (4 percent). Twenty-five percent of the youths reported one, and 26 percent reported two or more of these physical harm experiences. The 1995 national survey on family violence (Straus et al., 1998) found parent-to-child violence prevalence rates for being hit with something (5 percent), beat up (0.6 percent), or threatened with a knife or gun (0.1 percent), which were far lower than those reported by the youths we interviewed.

Sexual Victimization

Drawing upon the work of Finkelhor (1979), we asked the youths about their sexual experiences. They were asked about experiences such as showing or being shown sex organs, touching of sex organs, or intercourse, and how many experiences they had. Consistent with Finkelhor's (1979) operational definition, youths aged thirteen or under at the time of a sexual experience with a person over age eighteen were considered to have been sexually victimized. Youths of any age who had been forced or threatened; were afraid or shocked; or had a sexual experience with their parent, stepparent, or grandparent were also considered to have been sexually victimized. In line with this operational definition, consenting relationships between youths aged fourteen to seventeen years and an adult would not be classified as sexual abuse. Overall, 25 percent of the youths had been sexually victimized at least once in their lives (34 percent of the females and 18 percent of the males, chi-square = 10.29, df = 1, $p < .001$). These rates are similar to the rates reported by youths involved in a longitudinal study of juvenile detainees in Tampa (Dembo, Williams, and Schmeidler, 1998). The rate of sexual victimization among females is comparable to the rate Mouzakitis (1981) found among the Arkansas training school girls he studied.

Friends' Substance Use and Involvement with Police or Courts

Fifty-six percent of the youths noted that during the year prior to their baseline interview one or more of their close friends had used alcohol, 50 percent marijuana/hashish, 14 percent hallucinogens, and 7 percent cocaine. Further, many of their close friends had some type of contact with the legal system. Many youths reported that one of their close friends had been arrested (66 percent), held in jail or detention (52 percent), adjudicated delinquent or convicted of a crime (46 percent), put on community control or probation (43 percent), or sent to a training school or prison (15 percent).

Self-Reported Alcohol and Illicit-Drug Use Prior to Baseline Interview

Questions on substance use were adopted from the 1985 National Household Survey on Drug Abuse (NHSDA; National Institute on Drug Abuse, 1985). The questions sought to determine the youths' use of various categories of substances: tobacco, alcohol, marijuana/hashish in blunt form (in hollowed-out cigars) or in nonblunt form (e.g., reefer), inhalants, hallucinogens, cocaine, heroin, and the nonmedical use of barbiturates and other sedatives, tranquilizers, stimulants, and analgesics.

Alcohol Use

The youths' reported number of times being drunk or very high on alcohol formed a key measure of their involvement with this drug. As Table 3.5 shows, at their baseline interview 20 percent of the youths reported they had gotten very high or drunk on alcohol twelve or more days in the preceding twelve months. (In answer to another alcohol use question, 35 percent of the youths reported they never used alcohol.)

TABLE 3.5. Youths Reported Frequency of Getting Very High or Drunk on Alcohol in the Twelve Months Prior to Baseline Interview (n = 315)

Frequency	%
None	54
One or two days	11
Three to five days	7
Every other month or so (or six to eleven days)	8
One to two times a month (or twelve to twenty-four days a year)	7
Several times a month (or twenty-five to fifty-one days a year)	3
About one or two days a week	5
Almost daily or three to six days a week	4
Daily	1
Total	**100**

Use of Other Drugs

Our various analyses concerning the youths' illicit-drug use or nonmedical use of psychotherapeutic drugs focused on the frequency of their use of these drugs. At the time of their baseline interview, over half (56 percent) of the youths reported using marijuana/hashish in nonblunt form, and almost as many (50 percent) in blunt form, one or more times during their lifetime. Lifetime use of hallucinogens was reported by 14 percent of the youths, and 12 percent reported using cocaine. No other drug was used by more than 8 percent of the youths. Table 3.6 presents these results.

Seventeen percent of the youths reported using marijuana/hashish in nonblunt form, and 13 percent in blunt form, 100 or more times in their life. Because the reported lifetime frequency of marijuana/hashish use in nonblunt form and in blunt form was strongly associated $r = .667$, n = 315, $p < .001$), a composite index of the youths' marijuana/hashish use was created by summing standardized scores for these two variables. With the exception of these two forms of marijuana, youths who used one or two times accounted for about half of all users of each of the drugs. This demonstrates that, with the exception of marijuana, many youths reported being experimental, rather than systematic, users of drugs.

TABLE 3.6. Youths' Reported Lifetime Frequency of Drug Use Prior to Baseline Interview

Drug	Never Used (%)	Used 1 or 2 Times (%)	Used 3 to 5 Times (%)	Used 6 to 10 Times (%)	Used 11 to 49 Times (%)	Used 50 to 99 Times (%)	Used 100 to 199 Times (%)	Used 200 or More Times (%)	Total (n = 314 or 315) (%)
Marijuana/hashish (not blunts)	44	9	6	5	15	4	4	13	100
Blunts	50	10	7	7	9	4	4	9	100
Inhalants	92	4	2	2	*	*	–	–	100
Hallucinogens	86	6	2	2	3	1	–	–	100
Cocaine	88	6	1	1	2	1	*	*	99
Heroin	98	1	*	–	*	*	–	–	99
Nonmedical use of									
Stimulants	93	3	*	*	1	*	*	*	97
Sedatives	97	2	*	–	–	–	*	–	99
Tranquilizers	93	4	1	–	–	–	–	–	98
Analgesics	96	2	*	*	*	–	–	–	98

*Less than 1%

The drug use prevalence rates were, with one exception (the non-medical use of analgesics), higher than those reported by youths aged twelve to seventeen who were interviewed, for example, in the 1996 National Household Survey on Drug Abuse (Substance Abuse and Mental Health Services Administration, 1997). The rates reported in Table 3.6 compare with the NHSDA prevalence rates for nine categories of illicit drugs (given in parentheses) as follows: marijuana/hashish (in blunt or nonblunt form)—61 percent (versus 17 percent in the NHSDA sample); inhalants—8 percent (versus 6 percent); hallucinogens—14 percent (versus 6 percent); cocaine—12 percent (versus 2 percent); heroin—2 percent (versus 0. 5 percent); and nonmedical use of sedatives—3 percent (versus 1 percent); tranquilizers—7 percent (versus 2 percent); stimulants—7 percent (versus 2 percent); and analgesics— 4 percent (versus 6 percent).

Self-Reported Delinquent Behavior

Drawing upon the work of Elliott et al. (1983), we probed the youths' delinquent behavior in the year prior to their baseline interview by asking how many times they engaged in twenty-three delinquent behaviors. In addition, youths reporting they had engaged in a given act ten or more times were asked to indicate how often they participated in this behavior (once a month, once every two or three weeks, once a week, two to three times a week, once a day, or two to three times a day). In addition, for each of the twenty-three delinquent behaviors in which the youth claimed to have engaged, he or she was asked the age at which the act first occurred.

Based on the youths' claimed frequency of participation in the various delinquent acts, we calculated the following four summary indices of the youngsters' delinquent involvement as used by Elliott and his associates (1983):

- *General theft:* stole a motor vehicle, stole something worth more than $50, bought stolen goods, stole something worth less than $5, stole something worth between $5 and $50, broke into a building or vehicle, joyriding.
- *Crimes against persons:* aggravated assault, gang fights, hit a teacher, hit a parent, hit a student, sexual assault, strong-armed students, strong-armed teachers, strong-armed others.

- *Index crimes:* aggravated assault, sexual assault, gang fights, stole a motor vehicle, stole something worth more than $50, broke into a building or vehicle, strong-armed students, strong-armed teachers, strong-armed others.
- *Total delinquency:* the sum of the reported frequency of participation in the twenty-three delinquent activities.

In addition, we constructed a drug sales index for analysis as follows:

- *Drug sales:* sold marijuana or hashish, sold cocaine or crack, sold other hard drugs such as heroin or LSD.

The frequency rates for self-reported delinquency for the 315 youths during the year prior to their baseline interview indicated high prevalence rates for index offenses (57 percent), crimes against persons (70 percent), general theft (82 percent), drug sales (26 percent), and total delinquency (94 percent). Further, from 2 to 15 percent of the youths reported engaging in the offenses represented by the various scales 100 times or more—some reported many hundreds of offenses. Table 3.7 presents these results. For each of the indices, except total delinquency, youths who reported one to four offenses accounted for about half of all youths reporting offenses. Thus, many of the youths reported minimal, rather than substantial, involvement in some types of offenses.

Emotional/Psychological Functioning

The Symptom Check List-90-Revised (SCL-90-R) (Derogatis, 1983) was used to assess the youths' emotional/psychological functioning. The youths' replies to the items yielded T scores on nine symptom dimensions:

1. *Somatization*—distress arising from perceptions of bodily dysfunction
2. *Obsessive-compulsive*—symptoms that are closely identified with the standard clinical syndrome of the same name
3. *Interpersonal sensitivity*—feelings of personal inadequacy and inferiority, particularly in comparisons with others

4. *Depression*—a broad range of manifestations of clinical depression
5. *Anxiety*—a set of symptoms and signs that are associated clinically with high levels of manifest anxiety
6. *Hostility*—thoughts, feelings, or actions that are characteristic of the negative affect state of anger
7. *Phobic anxiety*—persistent fear of a specific person, place, object, or situation, characterized as irrational and disproportionate to the stimulus, leading to avoidance or escape behavior
8. *Paranoid ideation*—a disoriented mode of thinking
9. *Psychoticism*—includes a range of items tapping functioning from mild interpersonal alienation to dramatic evidence of psychosis

The *T* score means of the nine SCL-90-R scales were all 47.2 or lower. Comparison to the mean of 50 and standard deviation of 10 in the standardizing population (adolescent nonpatients) indicated the *T* scores for the nine scales were significantly lower than the scores for the standardizing population at the .001 significance level. On each scale, a low score indicates fewer symptoms.

Hair Testing for Substance Use

An important part of the youths' interviews was obtaining hair specimens for analysis for recent drug use. About one and a half inches of hair were collected across a finger and cut as close to the scalp as possible. The hair specimens were prepared for shipment following the established protocol of Psychemedics Corporation in Culver City, California, and processed by them.

Psychemedics performed radioimmunoassay (RIAH) testing of the hair samples for use in the past 90 days of the following substances: cocaine, opiates, PCP, methamphetamines, and marijuana. The cutoff for a positive result for cocaine and methamphetamines was 5 ng/10 mg hair; for PCP it was 3 ng/10 mg of hair; for opiates it was 2 ng/10 mg of hair; and for marijuana it was 10 pg carboxy—THC equivalents/10 mg of hair. (In a few cases in which hair was not available, fingernail samples were collected and analyzed.) In the case of cocaine and opiates, the antibody used in the radioimmunoassay does not produce any false positive results. With the marijuana radioimmunoassay, 5 to 10 percent of positive results may be false

TABLE 3.7. Self-Reported Delinquency in Twelve Months Prior to Baseline Interview (n = 315)

Index/Behavior	0 (%)	1-4 (%)	5-29 (%)	30-54 (%)	55-99 (%)	100-199 (%)	200+ (%)	Total (%)
Index Offenses	43	31	18	4	2	2	*	100
Crimes Against Persons	30	37	24	4	3	2	1	101
General Theft	18	38	28	7	4	3	2	100
Drug Sales	74	10	8	2	*	1	4	99
Total Delinquency	6	28	36	10	5	4	11	100

*Less than 1%

positives as a result of hair matrix effects near the cutoff level of the assay. False negatives are determined by the values of the cutoff level. For cocaine, individuals using fewer than one to three lines of cocaine per month are reported as negative. For opiates, individuals using fewer than two bags of heroin per week are scored as negative. For marijuana, because of its 100,000 lower concentration in hair than cocaine, only the heavy or moderate, but not the light, user, is identified by the hair assay. The exact clinical definitions of these categories of use have not been defined to date (Baumgartner and Hill, 1996).

The results of the hair testing were striking. Forty-five percent of the 298 youths tested (no test results were available for seventeen youths) were positive on one or more of the five drugs: 32 percent were positive on one drug (marijuana [22 percent] or cocaine [9 percent]), 13 percent were positive on two drugs (marijuana and cocaine [12 percent], marijuana and opiates [1 percent]), and 1 percent were positive on marijuana, cocaine, and opiates. Overall, 36 percent of the youths were positive on marijuana and 22 percent were positive on cocaine.

Comparison between hair test and self-reported drug use in the past three months showed remarkably different results for marijuana and cocaine. For marijuana, 70 percent of youths who tested positive reported use, and 38 percent of youths with negative hair tests also reported recent use. These discrepancies may be attributable to errors in the hair testing (including insensitivity to light use of marijuana) or incorrect self-reports. For cocaine, only 12 percent of the youths who tested positive reported use, and 5 percent of the youths who tested negative also reported recent use. Since false positive hair tests for cocaine are very rare, the low rate of self-reported cocaine use may be attributable to reluctance to admit involvement in this relatively stigmatizing behavior. The low rate of reported cocaine use among youths who did not test positive is consistent with this explanation that youths tend not to report their cocaine use.

Development of Summary Measures

A wide range of information was collected on the youths during the course of the project. To facilitate various analyses, summary measures were developed for the following sets of variables:

1. Delinquency history
2. Family alcohol, other drug, and mental health problems and contact with the justice system
3. Friends' alcohol/other drug use and contact with the justice system
4. Self-reported physical abuse
5. Emotional/psychological functioning and self-reported delinquent behavior (The measure of sexual victimization was discussed earlier in this chapter.) These summary measures are briefly defined in Table 3.8 and discussed in more detail in Appendix A.

TABLE 3.8. Summary Measures of Major Youth Baseline Variables

Measure	Definition
Delinquency referral history	Two factor-analysis based summary measures: (1) violence, property, and public disorder offenses and (2) drug offenses.
Family problems	Two factor-analysis based summary measures: (1) family alcohol, other drug, and mental health problems and (2) family involvement with the justice system.
Friends' problem behavior	Two factor-analysis based summary measures: (1) friends' drug use and (2) friends' involvement with the justice system.
Self-reported physical abuse	Two factor-analysis based summary measures: (1) serious physical harm—been beaten with something "hard" (e.g., club), been injured with a weapon, been hurt badly enough to need bandages or a doctor, spent time in a hospital because physically injured and (2) been beaten or hit.
Self-reported delinquent behavior	Five log-transformed, summary measures reflecting youths' involvement in general theft crimes, crimes against persons, index offenses, drug sales, and total delinquency—with no offenses coded as −1.
Emotional/psychological functioning	One factor-analysis based summary measure of the nine SCL-90-R scale *T* scores.

SUMMARY

Information collected on youths entering the Youth Support Project indicates that many of them were experiencing difficulties in the areas of delinquency, physical abuse, sexual victimization, emotional/psychological functioning, educational functioning, and alcohol and other drug use. In addition, many youths lived in families whose members had experienced problems with alcohol/other drug use, mental health, or the justice system. Importantly, although the youths' self-reports and hair test results indicate high levels of drug use, particularly the use of marijuana and cocaine, few youths had been arrested on drug-related charges. Further, the results of the hair tests for past ninety-day drug use indicate a much higher rate of cocaine use (22 percent) than the youths' reported lifetime use of this drug (12 percent).

Chapter 4

Impact of the Family Empowerment Intervention on Crime

Policymakers have been particularly interested in the effect on delinquency and crime rates of juvenile offender services and intervention programs. Their need for empirical documentation of the outcomes of these programs, and cost-effectiveness, is likely to increase in the future as competition for public funds to address various social needs increases. Accordingly, a major focus of our evaluation of the Youth Support Project (YSP) was on the impact of the Family Empowerment Intervention (FEI) on crime among youths involved in the project. The FEI was designed to be an intensive, but brief (ten weeks) intervention. Hence, it was important to learn if the intervention had positive effects that lasted for at least a year. We were also interested in whether the intervention had longer term positive effects indicating that it had a sustained impact on youths' behavior (Center for the Study and Prevention of Violence, 1999). We used self-report and official record data to examine both short- and long-term outcomes.

The short-term outcome analyses involving official record data focused on the number of new charges and new arrests in the twelve months following random assignment to the FEI or Extended Services Intervention (ESI) group. The long-term studies of official record data on the youths covered twelve to forty-eight months following their random assignment to the FEI or ESI group. The official record data analyses involved 303 youths entering the project between September 1, 1994, and December 31, 1997. The outcome analyses involving the youths' self-reported data studied the number of new delinquent behaviors in the five areas of delinquent behavior (general theft, crimes against persons, index crimes, drug sales, and total delinquency) discussed in Chapter 3. The short-term self-report data analyses covered twelve months following the youths' baseline interviews. The long-term self-report data analyses covered up to thirty-six months following the youths' baseline interviews. The self-reported delinquency/crime data analyses involved 278 of 315 eligible youths who entered the project between September 1, 1994, and January 31, 1998.

CASE TYPE

The Juvenile Assessment Center's (JAC's) misdemeanor case management unit reviews the arrest histories and current charges of youths arrested on misdemeanor offenses to determine their eligibility for involvement in a nonjudicial diversion program: arbitration or the Juvenile Alternative Services Program (JASP). Youths meeting the criteria for arbitration or JASP are referred to a case manager for that program; the case managers' recommendations are forwarded to the state's attorney's office for approval. (The youths tend to have offense histories, if any, involving minor offenses, such as retail theft.) Experience indicates the vast majority of the case managers' recommendations are approved by the state's attorney's office. Admission of guilt is required for a youth to be accepted into either diversion program.

Arbitration is a short-term program involving a trained arbitrator (not a judge), who hears the case against a youth and obtains relevant information from the youth, victim, and arresting officer. On the basis of this information, the arbitrator decides on sanctions against the youth. These sanctions can include community service, participation in a counseling program, paying restitution, or a combination of these sanctions. On average, youths complete the arbitration program in ten weeks. The JASP is a ninety-day program that imposes immediate sanctions on misdemeanor offenders. The program has a number of components: community service (youths are assigned to complete a number of community service hours), victim restitution, and counseling (short-term individual, adolescent group, and family counseling). The JASP counselors monitor youths' fulfillment of their required sanctions.

We scored the youths' designation as a nonserious offender (diversion-eligible case) or more serious offender (nondiversion case) at each youth's entry into the project. Overall, 38 percent of the 303 youths entering the YSP by December 31, 1997, had been recommended to receive diversion services; 62 percent had been referred to juvenile court. Fifty-seven of the 303 youths (19 percent) were diversion cases who also received FEI services. For our analyses, we created a case type variable with 1 indicating a diversion case, and 0 for all other cases, among the YSP youths. We were also interested in examining whether youths with nonserious offense histories benefited more from FEI services, as reflected in lower delinquency/crime over time, than youths with more serious offense records. To this end, we created a variable reflecting the interaction of case type and assignment to the FEI or ESI group on the youths' official record and self-reported delinquency/crime. The interaction effect of ESI or FEI group assignment and case type was created with 1 for diversion-eligible FEI youths and 0 for all other youths. This variable was included in the short-term official record and self-reported delinquency/crime analyses. When the interaction variable defined in this way is included in stepwise regression analyses after including the effects of case type and group assignment, it assesses interaction defined in the usual analysis-of-variance fashion: Is there a difference between the effects of treatment on the diversion and nondiversion youths? (This interaction may also be interpreted as: Is there a difference between the effects of case type for the FEI and ESI youths?)

OFFICIAL RECORD OUTCOMES

For the official record analyses, we obtained records of contact with the juvenile justice system; adult arrests recorded in the information systems of the Florida Department of Law Enforcement, the Hillsborough County Jail System, and the State's Attorney of Hillsborough County; and involvement with the Florida Department of Corrections for each youth during the twelve months following random assignment to the FEI or ESI group. For both short- and long-term results, two parallel analyses were completed using the official record data: (1) the number of offenses with which each youth was charged, and (2) the number of arrests each youth experienced.

Number of New Offenses

In line with previous research (Dembo et al., 1993; Dembo, Ramirez-Garnica, et al., 2001), we developed summary measures for the following offense categories:

1. *Violent felonies:* murder/manslaughter, robbery, sex offenses, aggravated assault
2. *Property felonies:* arson, burglary, auto theft, larceny/theft ($300 and over), stolen property, property damage
3. *Drug felonies:* drug offenses (e.g., cocaine possession)
4. *Violent misdemeanors:* nonaggravated assault
5. *Property misdemeanors:* larceny/theft, stolen property, property damage
6. *Drug misdemeanors:* drug offenses (e.g., possessing a small amount of marijuana)
7. *Public disorder misdemeanors:* public disorder, trespassing
8. *The total number of charges across these offense categories*

For all offense categories except total charges, if an offense was of indeterminate seriousness, it was scored as one-half in each of the corresponding felony and misdemeanor summary measures. Table 4.1 provides the youths' prevalence rates of being charged in the seven specific offense categories and total charges across these categories twelve, twenty-four, thirty-six, and forty-eight months following random assignment to the FEI or ESI group.

Within the first twelve months (Time 1), less than a quarter of the youths were charged with offenses in each of the seven offense-specific categories. On the other hand, nearly half (48 percent) of the youths were charged with one or more offenses during Time 1. As discussed below, the total charges variable had a respectable variance, making it a good candidate for further study. In contrast, the specific types of offenses were not analyzed in detail because few youths had charges for any specific offense. Because rates of charges generally declined from Time 1 to Time 4, the analysis of long-term charges focused on total charges.

TABLE 4.1. Percentage of Project Youths Who Were Charged One or More Times for Various Types of Offenses During the Forty-Eight Months of Follow-Up

Charged One or More Times for	Follow-Up Period After Random Assignment			
	Time 1: Within 12 Months (n = 303)	Time 2: Within the Second 12 Months (n = 193)	Time 3: Within the Third 12 Months (n = 118)	Time 4: Within the Fourth 12 Months (n = 23)
Violent felony offenses	14%	9%	4%	4%
Property felony offenses	15%	14%	13%	9%
Drug felony offenses	6%	7%	6%	9%
Violent misdemeanor offenses	17%	8%	2%	0%
Property misdemeanor offenses	24%	14%	9%	9%
Drug misdemeanor offenses	8%	6%	8%	9%
Public disorder misdemeanor offenses	14%	7%	7%	9%
Total charges	48%	37%	27%	17%

Number of New Arrests

Because a given arrest can involve multiple charges, we created a variable reflecting the total number of arrests (as a juvenile or as an adult) each youth experienced during Time 1 (score range: 0 to 9). A similar cumulative total of arrests over the twelve to forty-eight month period was calculated for each youth to assess long-term outcome. For both charges and arrests, youths with as few as twelve months of follow-up were included in these "long-term" outcome analyses.

Transformations of Data on New Charges and New Arrests

Before analyzing the number of new charges or arrests, we transformed the data for each measure separately. We used a square root transformation if there was any offense or arrest, rather than a logarithmic transformation because there were fewer charges or arrests than self-reported offenses. If there was a charge or arrest, we did not correct for time at risk (i.e., incarcerated in a juvenile detention center, jail, residential commitment program, prison, or other secure facility). Since reduced time at risk was almost invariably due to incarceration because of offenses, correction for time at risk would have penalized offenders twice. If there was no charge or arrest, the score was the negative of the square root of the years at risk. For example, no charge or arrest in twelve months was assigned the score –1. The resulting scores emphasize the difference between offenders and nonoffenders and deemphasize time at risk for nonoffenders. All offenders were assigned positive scores and all nonoffenders negative scores. For the first year, the means and standard deviations of the transformed scores were as follows:

Number of charges: mean = 0.31; standard deviation = 1.43
Number of arrests: mean = 0.17; standard deviation = 1.25

The Pearson correlation between the transformed numbers of charges and arrests was .985 for the first year. For the cumulative totals of one to four years, the means and standard deviations of the transformed scores were as follows:

Number of charges: mean = 2.22; standard deviation = 1.32
Number of arrests: mean = –0.06; standard deviation = 1.19

For the long-term official record outcomes, the correlation between the transformed number of charges and arrests was .987.

Short-Term Official Record Outcome

Analytic Strategy

The major focus of our analyses was to determine the impact of assignment to the FEI or ESI group, and secondarily, the interaction of case type by group assignment on the youths' official records of new charges and new arrests during the twelve months following random assignment to the FEI or ESI group (Time 1). Accordingly, we performed separate stepwise regression analyses on these two outcome measures with mean substitution for missing data on the predictor variables (Dembo, Ramirez-Garnica, et al., 2000).

Prior to conducting the regression analyses, we completed a principal components analysis on twenty-three of the youths' baseline psychosocial, delinquency and dependency referral history, and abuse-neglect history variables. Highly skewed variables with little variance (e.g., referral history for status offenses, substance abuse treatment history) were excluded from this analysis and thus did not contribute to the regression analyses. Seven principal components with eigenvalues greater than 1.0 were identified among these twenty-three predictor variables, and they accounted for 54 percent of the variance. Further, the communalities of the variables across the seven principal components were sizable. The seven principal components were varimax rotated for factor clarity. Based on the loadings, the seven varimax-rotated factors reflect drug use, referral history for neglect, psychosocial problems, drug offense history, property offense arrest at entering the JAC, referral history for physical abuse, and having been seriously physically abused (Dembo, Ramirez-Garnica, et al., 2000). Summary regression factor scores (Kim and Mueller, 1978) on these seven varimax-rotated factors, together with the youths' demographic characteristics (age, race, gender, ethnicity, and living situation), the youths' number of delinquency referrals prior to entering the project, case type, group assignment, and case type by group assignment, were included as predictor variables in the regression analyses. Principal components analysis is a standard treatment for potential collinearity problems among predictors (Draper and Smith, 1980). In addition, it averages out to some degree the measurement error of predictors, if any, and thus diminishes error-in-variable problems. The inclusion of the seven varimax-rotated factors as predictors in a regression analysis has the same effect as including the seven principal components.

Our main purpose in completing the multiple regression analyses was to control for any group differences in the (baseline) predictor variables, noted above, before examining the effect of FEI (coded 1) or ESI (coded 0) group assignment. (Another purpose in controlling for the baseline predictors was to reduce within-group variation in outcome associated with within-group differences in the baseline variables. The significance of the baseline predictors confirmed that this purpose was achieved for each outcome variable.) In the interest of conserving space, the detailed results of these regression analyses are not presented here. They can be found in Dembo, Ramirez-Garnica, et al. (2000). Our primary purpose in these outcome analyses was to test the efficacy of the FEI in comparison with the ESI, which served as a less-intensive control intervention. Therefore, we used a one-sided test for the group assignment variable. A secondary interest was to ascertain whether there was an interaction effect involving case type by group assignment on the various official record outcome measures. Reflective of these interests, we entered the baseline predictor variables in a single step in each stepwise analysis, followed by the FEI or ESI group assignment variable, and then the case type by group assignment interaction term.

Predicting Total Number of New Arrest Charges

The summary results of the stepwise multiple regression analysis predicting the youths' total number of charges across the seven offense categories during Time 1 are presented in Table 4.2. The baseline predictors as a group had $R^2 = 0.358$. In contrast, the R^2 change (.003) associated with the FEI-ESI group assignment variable was quite low and nonsignificant. A low and nonsignificant R^2 change value (0.003) was also associated with the case type by group assignment variable in regard to total arrest charges. Overall, the predictor variables accounted for 36.4 percent of the variance.

Predicting Total Number of New Arrests

The results of the stepwise multiple regression analysis predicting the youths' total number of arrests across the seven offense categories during Time 1 are also shown in Table 4.2. The baseline predictors had $R^2 = 0.364$. The R^2 change (.002) associated with the FEI-ESI group assignment variable was low and nonsignificant. A low and nonsignificant R^2 change value (.003) was also associated with the case type by group assignment variable in regard to total arrests. Overall, the predictor variables accounted for 36.9 percent of the variance.

TABLE 4.2. Results of Regression Analyses Involving New Arrest Charges and New Arrests During Time 1 (n = 303)

Variables	R^2 (14 Baseline (Characteristics)	R^2 Change FEI vs. ESI	R^2 Change Case Type × Group Assignment	Overall R^2
New arrest charges	.358***	.003	.003	.364***
New arrests	.364***	.002	.003	.369***

Note: Group-assignment significance levels were for a one-sided test. All other significance levels were not directional.
* .10 > p > .05
** p < .05
*** p < .01
**** p < .001

Does Completion of the FEI Make a Difference in Outcome?

Fifty-three percent of 149 youths and families receiving FEI services completed the intervention (n = 79), but the other 47 percent (n = 70) did not. The decision not to continue receiving FEI services was made by the family or was necessitated by the absence of the client youth. Field consultants did not close any case due to a client youth's arrest or development of a drug problem. On the contrary, these issues were considered important areas to address within the intervention and through appropriate referrals to community programs. In many cases, families moved out of the area or the parents/guardians were not willing or able to continue participating in the family meetings.

A discriminant analysis comparing the FEI cases that did and did not complete the intervention found no overall significant difference between them on fourteen baseline variables (seven psychosocial, delinquency history, and abuse-neglect history varimax factors and seven sociodemographic and referral history variables) (Wilks' lambda = 0.909, chi-square = 13.34, df = 14, p = n.s.). In addition, there was no significant difference between the two groups on any of the comparison variables. Since the sample sizes were small, and to simplify presentation of results, these two subgroups of FEI cases were compared using one-sided *t* tests, without controlling for baseline characteristics. Table 4.3 presents these results and also displays the ESI group results for comparison.

As shown in Table 4.3, statistically significant differences were found for the two outcome variables (total number of new charges and total number of new arrests). Youths completing the FEI had significantly *lower* rates of new charges and significantly *fewer* new arrests than youths not completing the FEI. These important effects are presented graphically in Figures 4.1 and 4.2, which display the mean values for the transformed total number of new charges (Figure 4.1) and transformed total number of new arrests (Figure 4.2) for ESI youths, youths not completing the FEI, and youths completing the FEI during Time 1. The ESI youths, on average, had 0.41 new charges compared to 0.53 new charges for youths not completing the FEI and –0.09 new charges for youths completing the FEI. Further, ESI youths, on average, had 0.25 new arrests, compared to 0.40 new arrests for youths not completing the FEI and –0.19 new arrests for youths completing the FEI.

TABLE 4.3. Comparison of Transformed Official Record Outcome Measures Across ESI Youths, Youths Not Completing the FEI, and Youths Completing the FEI

Outcome Measure	ESI Youths (n = 154)	Youths Not Completing the FEI (n = 70)	Youths Completing the FEI (n = 79)	*t* Value of Not Completing vs. Completing
Total number of new charges	.41	.53	–.09	2.77*** (df = 147)
Total number of new arrests	.25	.40	–.19	2.95*** (df = 147)

Note: The variables used in these analyses were coded so that the higher the score, the more recidivism reflected in the measure.
*.10 > p > .05
**p < .05
***p < .01
****p < .001—*t* test one-sided significance levels

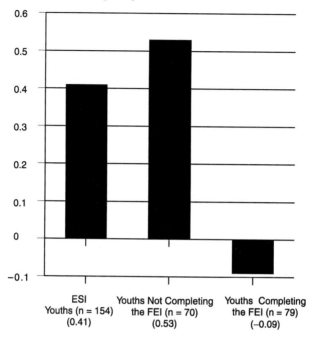

FIGURE 4.1. Mean Transformed Number of New Arrest Charges for ESI Youths, Youths Not Completing the FEI, and Youths Completing the FEI: Time 1

Long-Term Official Record Outcomes

As in our analyses of official record outcomes in Time 1, the main comparison groups of interest in our analyses of long-term official record outcomes were ESI youths (n = 154), youths not completing the FEI (n = 70), and youths completing the FEI (n = 79). Case type did not prove useful in the short-term analyses, so we did not include it in our long-term outcome analyses.

Comparison of the Three Groups at Entry

A discriminant analysis was completed comparing the three groups on fourteen entry variables (the seven psychosocial, delinquency history, and abuse-neglect history varimax components and the seven sociodemographic and referral history variables [age, gender, race, ethnicity, living situation, diversion or other case, and total number of

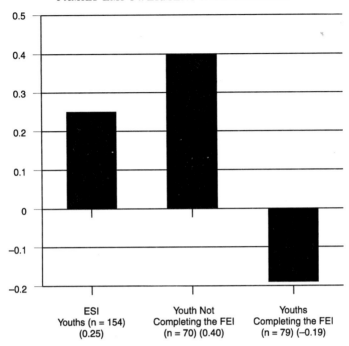

FIGURE 4.2. Mean Transformed Number of New Arrests for ESI Youths, Youths Not Completing the FEI, and Youths Completing the FEI: Time 1

previous delinquency referrals]). The results were as follows: Wilks' lambda = 0.892, chi-square = 33.65, df = 26, p = n.s. (function 1); Wilks' lambda = 0.970, chi-square = 9.08, df = 12, p = n.s. (function 2). In addition, there was no significant difference among the three groups on any of the variables. Based on these results, we did not deem it necessary to control statistically for possible differences at entry among these groups before examining the impact of the intervention on the youths' number of new charges and new arrests.

*Cumulative New Charges and New Arrests
for the Three Groups*

For each of the comparisons among groups—FEI versus ESI, FEI completers versus FEI noncompleters, and FEI completers against all others—two-way analyses of variance (ANOVAs) were performed.

One independent variable was the group difference of interest, the other was the number of years of follow-up. This two-way ANOVA removes variation associated with length of follow-up from the comparison of groups. Table 4.4 presents results of the ANOVAs for these comparisons.

Using transformed variables that adjusted for time at risk for nonoffenders, FEI youths had fewer charges and arrests than ESI youths. A further indication of the impact of the FEI was that youths who completed the FEI had fewer charges and arrests than those who did not complete the FEI. In an additional comparison, youths who did not complete the FEI together with ESI youths had more charges and arrests than youths who completed the FEI. All differences between groups shown in Table 4.4 were in the predicted direction, and the

TABLE 4.4. Comparison of Cumulative Recidivism Measures Across ESI Youths, Youths Not Completing the FEI, and Youths Completing the FEI

	df	Transformed Charges				Transformed Arrests			
		SS	MS	F	p	SS	MS	F	p
FEI vs. ESI	1	.11	.11	.04	.423	.00	.00	.00	.00
Years of follow-up	3	27.10	9.03	3.09	.027	13.74	4.58	1.99	.116
Interaction	3	8.20	2.73	.94	.424	7.66	2.55	1.11	.346
Error	295	862.06	2.92			679.39	2.30		
FEI Completed vs. FEI Not Completed	1	5.47	5.47	1.93	.083	6.27	6.27	2.71	.051
Years of follow-up	3	17.49	5.83	2.06	.108	12.25	4.08	1.77	.156
Interaction	3	12.17	4.06	1.43	.235	9.13	3.04	1.32	.271
Error	141	399.10	2.83			325.84	2.31		
FEI Completed vs. All Other Youths	1	2.50	2.50	.86	.177	2.15	2.15	.93	.168
Years of follow-up	3	28.20	9.40	3.23	.023	16.03	5.34	2.32	.075
Interaction	3	5.84	1.95	.67	.572	3.95	1.32	.57	.633
Error	295	859.52	2.91			678.47	2.30		

Note: The variables used in these analyses were coded as follows: for the total number of arrest charges and total number of arrests, higher scores indicate more recidivism reflected in the measure. Tests of differences between groups were one-sided. Other tests were not directional.

FEI youths who completed the intervention had marginally significantly fewer transformed charges ($F = 1.93$; df = 1,141; $p = .083$—one-sided) and very close to significantly fewer transformed arrests ($F = 2.71$; df = 1,141; $p = .05$—one-sided) than youths not completing the FEI.

Figures 4.3 and 4.4 display the mean values for transformed new charges (Figure 4.3) and transformed new arrests (Figure 4.4) for ESI youths, youths not completing the FEI, and youths completing the FEI. As can be seen, ESI youths, on average, had 0.71 new charges compared to 0.67 new charges for youths not completing the FEI and 0.36 new charges for youths completing the FEI. Further, ESI youths, on average, had 0.49 new arrests compared to 0.52 new arrests for youths not completing the FEI and 0.20 new arrests for youths completing the FEI.

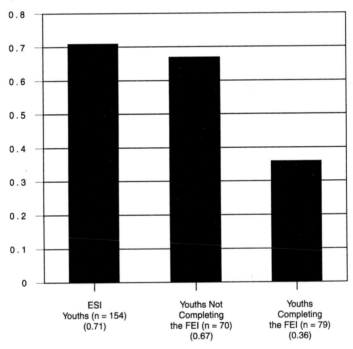

FIGURE 4.3. Mean Transformed Number of New Arrest Charges for ESI Youths, Youths Not Completing the FEI, and Youths Completing the FEI: Long-Term Outcome

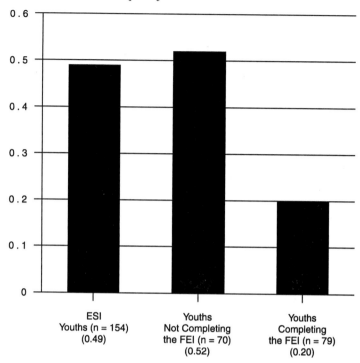

FIGURE 4.4. Mean Transformed Number of New Arrests for ESI Youths, Youths Not Completing the FEI, and Youths Completing the FEI: Long-Term Outcome

Time and Treatment Group by Time Effects on the Recidivism Measures

The two-way analyses of variance also assessed the effect of length of follow-up time on the number of charges and arrests and the interaction between each of the three pairs of comparison groups (defined in Table 4.4) over time in regard to total number of charges and arrests, respectively. Statistically significant increases in number of charges and arrests from Time 1 to Time 4 (in the analyses for all youths) reflect a cumulative increase from Time 1 to Time 4, despite the mitigating effect of the transformation. This contrasts with the results in Table 4.1, which showed a general decline in additional charges in each year from Time 1 to Time 4. However, no statistically significant interaction effects were found for any pair of comparison groups by time for either recidivism measure. The absence of interaction effects may be interpreted as indicating that in each analysis, the pairs of comparison groups did not differ significantly in their charges over time.

Summary of Official Record Outcomes

The results of our short-term official record outcome analyses indicate that the FEI and ESI youths did not differ significantly in their total number of new charges and total number of new arrests during Time 1. However, statistically significant differences were found for youths not completing the FEI and youths completing the FEI. Youths completing the FEI had significantly lower rates of new charges and new arrests than youths not completing the FEI.

Comparison of youths who did and did not complete the FEI shows clearly that the intervention was successful only for those youths who completed it. The ESI youths usually had fewer crimes than the noncompleters and more than the completers, but they were more similar to the noncompleters. An alternative explanation is that youths did better because they were amenable to intervention, rather than as the effect of the intervention. However, if this was so, one would expect that there would be other differences in baseline characteristics, which we did not find to be the case.

In our long-term analyses, the results indicate that youths completing the FEI had marginally significantly lower cumulative arrest charges and very close to statistically significant lower cumulative new arrests over Time 1 to Time 4 than youths not competing the FEI. These results support the efficacy of the FEI, although at a more modest level than in the Time 1 analyses. Again, an alternative explanation is that youths did better because they were amenable to intervention, but we did not find other differences in baseline characteristics to support that explanation.

Since the intervention was designed to be short-term, and no additional services were systematically provided following completion of the FEI, the long-term outcomes we found were gratifying. We believe the strength of the long-term effect of the FEI could have been enhanced by periodic booster sessions designed to support maintenance of the intervention gains made by client youths and their families. The long-term recidivism findings are particularly important in light of experience showing that the salutary effects of intervention programs for high-risk youths are, unfortunately, often short-lived. The Center for the Study and Prevention of Violence (1999) reports that the treatment or intervention gains of most programs are lost after participation in the intervention or soon thereafter. The intervention effects we found are consistent with the main hypothesis of this project. Further, as we discuss in Chapter 7, substantial direct cost savings can be anticipated for the justice system from using this intervention.

SELF-REPORTED DELINQUENCY

Analytic Strategy

Our analyses of the youths' self-reports of involvement in delinquency/crime focused on the youths' involvement in general theft offenses, crimes against persons, index crimes, drug sales, and total delinquency. Our major focus in the Time 1 outcome analyses of these data was to determine the impact of assignment to the FEI or ESI group on the youths' reported involvement in delinquent behavior. Accordingly, five separate stepwise regression analyses were performed (Dembo, Seeberger, et al., 2000).

Two hundred and seventy-two youths were involved in these analyses. A discriminant analysis (Bennett and Bowers, 1976; Klecka, 1980) was performed comparing the 272 youths for whom we had baseline interview and follow-up interview data with the forty-three youths in the study who did not complete Time 1 follow-up interviews. Our purpose was to learn if there were any important differences between the two groups in their baseline demographic, psychosocial, and delinquency and dependency referral characteristics. The results indicated that, overall, the two groups were not significantly different from one another on these variables (chi-square test of Wilks' lambda = 39.92, df = 31, p = n.s.). For youths entering the project through December 31, 1997 (n = 303), additional analyses compared these two groups on official records of new charges and new arrests, adjusting for time at risk among youths with no offenses. The results showed the 263 youths with follow-up interview data had significantly more new charges (t = 2.27, df = 301, p = .024) and more new arrests ($t = 2.20$, df $= 301$, $p = .028$) than the forty youths without follow-up interview data. This discrepancy may be due to the limitation of official records from the State of Florida.

Prior to conducting the regression analyses, we conducted a principal components analysis on the twenty-three baseline psychosocial, offense history, and abuse-neglect history variables discussed previously. This analysis identified eight principal components with eigenvalues greater than 1.0 that accounted for 58 percent of the variance. These clusters were varimax rotated for factor clarity. The varimax-rotated factors reflect drug use, delinquency history, psychosocial problems, drug offense history, property offenses at entering the JAC, having been hit or beaten, mental health treatment, and having been seriously physically abused. Regression factor scores (Kim and Mueller, 1978) of these eight varimax-rotated principal components, the youths' demographic characteristics (age, race, gender, ethnicity, and living situation), case type, group assignment, and case type by group assignment, were included as predictor variables in the various regression analyses.

The analytic strategy was informed by our primary interest in testing the efficacy of the FEI in comparison with the ESI. Hence, we used a one-sided test for the group assignment variable. A secondary interest was to learn whether there was an interaction effect involving case type by group assignment on the self-reported delinquency variables. Accordingly, as was the case for the official record outcome analyses, we entered the youths' baseline predictor variables in a single step in each stepwise analysis, followed by the FEI or ESI group assignment variable, and then the case type by group assignment interaction term.

Short-Term Self-Reported Delinquency

Compared to their baseline interview, at their first follow-up interview the youths reported generally lower prevalence rates of engaging in the offenses summarized by the five scales (index offenses, 42 percent; crimes against persons, 64 percent; general theft, 56 percent; drug sales, 29 percent; and total delinquency, 76 percent). From 1 percent to 16 percent of the 272 youths claimed to have engaged in the offenses represented by the various scales 100 or more times since their baseline interviews, and some youths reported many hundreds of delinquent acts.

The scoring of the self-reported delinquency follow-up data was complicated by the difference in time at risk. For every subject, time at risk could be ideally defined as the number of days in the community not in a secure facility. However, it was not feasible to determine this. This ideal variable could be expressed as the product of the number of days between the baseline interview and the follow-up interview times the proportion of those days in the community. The variable used in this study to represent the days at risk was the number of days between the two interviews times the proportion of days in the community in the 365 days following the baseline interview. If the follow-up interview was on the anniversary of the baseline interview, this would be the days at risk, ideally defined. Otherwise, it is a good approximation. The days at risk is divided by 365 to yield years at risk.

Different years-at-risk corrections were applied to the separate cases of one or more offenses versus no offenses. To correct a positive number of offenses, before taking the logarithm we divided it by years at risk. This gives the number of offenses that would have occurred at the same rate in 365 days at risk. (The years at risk ranged from 0.28 to 1.89; 70 percent of the years at risk were greater than 1.) If there was no offense, the assigned score, minus one in the study, was multiplied by the years at risk. This made the intensity of the negative score proportional to the length of time the youth remained free of offenses.

Validity of the Self-Reported Delinquency Data

In order to evaluate the accuracy of the youths' self-reported delinquency, we compared the total self-reported delinquency to the official record arrests in each follow-up period. It must be noted that if a youth had no official arrests, that does not invalidate reported delinquencies, since many delinquencies do not result in arrests. In contrast, if youths were arrested but reported no delinquencies, the validity of the denial of delinquency would be contradicted by the official record data. For the first follow-up period, 10 percent of the 133 youths with one or more arrests denied any delinquency. For the second and third follow-up periods, the comparable percentages were 20 percent of sixty-five arrested youths and 27 percent of twenty-six arrested youths. In contrast, among youths who were not arrested, the percentages who reported any delinquency were 57 percent, 58 percent, and 46 percent, respectively, in the three follow-up periods. These relatively low rates of denial of delinquency compared to the rates of admission of delinquency among youths who were not arrested suggest that most youths reported their delinquency accurately. Although the value of self-reports is reduced by denials that are invalidated by official records, admissions of involvement without official records outnumbered them substantially.

Predicting Self-Reported Delinquency

Separate multiple regression analyses were conducted for each of the five Time 1 self-reported delinquency measures discussed earlier. In addition to the various baseline predictor variables that were included in the analyses, we included the baseline counterpart of the Time 1 delinquency measure being studied. Table 4.5 presents these results.

TABLE 4.5. Results of Regression Analyses of Self-Reported Delinquency During Time 1 (n = 272)

Variable	R^2 (15 Baseline Characteristics)	R^2 Change: FEI vs. ESI	R^2 Change: Case Type × Group Assignment	Overall R^2
General Theft Offenses	.334****	.001	.001	.336****
Crimes Against Persons	.283****	.000	.001	.284****
Index Crimes	.352****	.000	.003	.355****
Drug Sales	.437****	.005*	.003	.445****
Total Delinquency	397****	.001	.000	.398****

Note: FEI vs. ESI significance levels were for a one-sided test. All other significance levels were not directional.
*.10 > p > .05
**p < .05
***p < .01
****p < .001

General theft offenses. The stepwise regression analysis predicting the youths' self-reported general theft offenses during Time 1 indicated that the baseline predictors had R^2 = 0.334. The R^2 change (.001) associated with the FEI-ESI group assignment variable was quite low and nonsignificant. A low and nonsignificant R^2 change value (.001) was also associated with the case type by group assignment interaction term. Overall, the predictor variables accounted for 33.6 percent of the variance.

Crimes against persons. The analysis predicting the youths' self-reported crimes against persons during Time 1 showed that the baseline predictors had R^2 = 0.283. The R^2 change (.000) associated with the FEI-ESI group assignment variable was quite low and nonsignificant, as was the R^2 change value (.001) associated with the case type by group assignment interaction term. Overall, the predictor variables accounted for 28.4 percent of the variance.

Index crimes. In the analysis predicting the youths' self-reported index crimes during Time 1, the baseline predictor variables had R^2 = 0.352. Again, the R^2 change (.000) associated with the FEI-ESI group assignment variable, and with the case type by group assignment interaction term (.003), was low and nonsignificant. Overall, the predictor variables accounted for 35.5 percent of the variance.

Drug sales. In the analysis predicting the youths' self-reported drug sales during Time 1, the baseline predictor variables had R^2 = 0.437. The R^2 change associated with the FEI-ESI group assignment variable was .005, which was marginally statistically significant (F = 2.15; df = 1,255; p = .07). The case type by group assignment interaction effect was low (R^2 change = .003) and nonsignificant. Overall, the predictor variables accounted for 44.5 percent of the variance.

After adjusting for the youths' baseline demographic, psychosocial, delinquency and dependency referral history, and their self-reported abuse experiences, the youths receiving FEI services had fewer drug sales than those receiving ESI services; the mean of the transformed variable was –0.42 compared to –0.24. Figure 4.5 depicts the mean values for the transformed drug sales measure for ESI youths, youths not completing the FEI, and youths completing the FEI. Youths completing the FEI had a mean of –0.75 compared to –0.11 for youths not completing the FEI.

Total delinquency. Table 4.5 also displays the results of the stepwise regression analysis predicting the youths' self-reported total de-

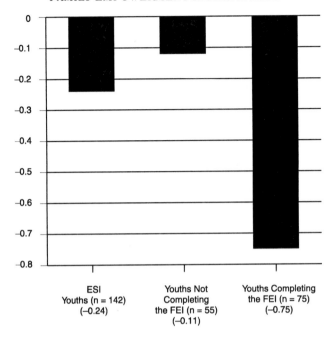

FIGURE 4.5. Adjusted Mean Values of Reported Drug Sales During Time 1 for ESI Youths, Youths Not Completing the FEI, and Youths Completing the FEI

linquency during Time 1. The baseline predictors variables had $R^2 =$ 0.397. The R^2 change (.001) associated with the FEI-ESI group assignment variable was quite low and nonsignificant, as was the R^2 change value (.000) associated with the case type by group assignment interaction term. Overall, the predictor variables accounted for 39.8 percent of the variance.

Does Completion of the FEI Make a Difference in Outcome?

Fifty-eight percent of 130 youths and families receiving FEI services completed the intervention but the other 42 percent of youths and families did not. A discriminant analysis comparing the FEI cases that did and did not complete the intervention found no overall significant difference between them on fourteen baseline variables (Wilks' lambda = 0.933, chi-square = 8.45, df = 14). In addition, there was no significant difference between the two groups on any of the comparison variables. Since the sample sizes were smaller, and to simplify the presentation of results, these two subgroups of FEI cases were compared using one-sided *t* tests. In contrast to the regression coefficients reported in the tables, these differences did not adjust for association with baseline characteristics. Table 4.6 presents these results and displays the ESI group results for comparison.

As can be seen, statistically significant differences were found between youths not completing the FEI and youths completing the FEI on self-reported crimes against persons ($p < .001$), drug sales ($p < .01$), and total delinquency ($p < .01$). Marginally statistically significant differences were found for self-reported general theft crimes and self-reported index crimes. In each case, youths completing the FEI had lower rates of delinquency.

TABLE 4.6. Comparison of Self-Reported Delinquency Outcome Measures Across ESI Youths, Youths Not Completing the FEI, and Youths Completing the FEI

Self-Reported Delinquency During the 12-Month Follow-up Period	ESI Youths (n = 142)	Youths Not Completing the FEI (n = 55)	Youths Completing the FEI (n = 75)	*t* Value of Not Completing vs. Completing
General theft crimes	.11	.09	−.18	1.45* (df = 128)
Crimes against persons	.01	.28	−.22	3.34**** (df = 128)
Index crimes	−.27	−.18	−.43	1.51* (df = 128)
Drug sales	−.24	−.11	−.75	2.96*** (df = 82.9)†
Total delinquency	.82	1.04	.33	3.37*** (df = 128)

Note: The variables used in these analyses were coded as follows: for the total number of arrest charges and total number of arrests, the higher the score, the more recidivism reflected in the measure, controlling for the youths' time at risk.
*$.10 > p > .05$
**$p < .05$
***$p < .01$
****$p < .001$—*t* test one-sided significance levels
† separate variance estimates *t* test

Long-Term Self-Reported Delinquency

As discussed in Chapter 3, depending on the date the youth entered the project, our long-term analyses of self-reported delinquency extended up to thirty-six months. Two hundred and seventy-eight youths were involved in these long-term outcome analyses: the 272 youths included in the Time 1 analyses plus six youths who were introduced at a second- or third-year follow-up (Dembo, Seeberger, et al., 2000). As we discussed in Chapter 3, we used the youths' self-reported delinquency information from the last available follow-up interview as the best measure of long-term outcome of this behavior. A discriminant analysis (Bennett and Bowers, 1976; Klecka, 1980) was performed comparing the 278 reinterviewees for whom we had baseline interview and last interview follow-up data to the other thirty-seven youths in the study with no follow-up data to learn if there were any important differences between the two groups on their baseline interview data and delinquency and dependency referral histories at entry into the project. The results indicated that, overall, the two groups were not significantly different from one another on these variables (chi-squared test of Wilks' lambda = 44.59, df = 32, p = n.s.).

Self-Reported Delinquency in the Year Prior
to Baseline Interview and During
the Last Follow-Up Period

As shown in Table 4.7, the 278 youths reported relatively high rates of delinquency during the year prior to their baseline interview. High prevalence rates were reported for index offenses (58 percent), crimes against persons (72 percent), general theft (82 percent), drug sales (25 percent), and total delinquency (94 percent). Further, from 2 to 16 percent of the youths reported engaging in the offenses represented by the various scales 100 times or more—some reported many hundreds of offenses. These self-reported delinquency scales were log transformed, as described for the Time 1 follow-up delinquency scales.

Table 4.7 also shows that at the time of their last follow-up interview, the youths reported lower prevalence rates of engaging in the offenses summarized by four of the five scales (index offenses, 33 percent; crimes against persons, 41 percent; general theft, 43 percent; and total delinquency, 66 percent). However, the prevalence rate for

TABLE 4.7. Self-Reported Delinquency (n = 278)

Index/Behavior	Frequency in Year Before Baseline Interview							
	0	1-4	5-29	30-54	55-99	100-199	200+	Total
Index offenses	42%	32%	17%	4%	2%	2%	<1%	99%
Crimes against person	28%	37%	25%	4%	3%	2%	1%	100%
General theft	18%	37%	27%	8%	4%	4%	2%	100%
Drug sales	75%	10%	7%	2%	<1%	1%	4%	99%
Total delinquency	6%	27%	37%	9%	5%	5%	11%	100%
	Frequency in Year Before Last Interview							
Index offenses	67%	19%	9%	2%	2%	<1%	<1%	99%
Crimes against person	58%	24%	13%	1%	1%	1%	1%	98%
General theft	56%	20%	15%	2%	1%	3%	2%	99%
Drug sales	72%	6%	8%	2%	1%	4%	7%	100%
Total delinquency	33%	21%	20%	5%	2%	5%	13%	99%

drug sales increased from 25 to 28 percent. From <1 percent to 18 percent of the 278 youths claimed to have engaged in the offenses represented by the various scales 100 or more times since their baseline interview, and some youths reported many hundreds of delinquent acts. These self-reported delinquency scales were log transformed and adjusted for time at risk in the same manner as the Time 1 follow-up delinquency scales. Comparing the frequencies of self-reported delinquency in the year prior to baseline interview and in the year before the last interview reveals significant decreases in all delinquency scales except drug sales, which increased.

Analytic Strategy

Prior to conducting the regression analyses of long-term self-reported delinquency, we completed the same principal components analysis on the youths' twenty-three baseline variables described previously in the section on short-term self-reported outcomes. Because our analyses of official record data indicated the importance of graduation from the FEI to outcome, our main interests in completing the multiple regression analyses were to control for the cumulative effect of various baseline predictor variables before examining the effect on outcome of (1) FEI (coded 1) or ESI (coded 0) group assignment and (2) a variable reflecting completion of the FEI. For each self-reported delinquency measure, we completed a separate regression analysis using the baseline predictor variables, including the varimax-rotated factors and demographic variables, plus the baseline counterpart of the specific delinquency measure being studied. To examine the effect of FEI completion on each delinquency outcome measure, we used a different variable for FEI completion in each analysis: the residual of a preliminary multiple regression predicting the FEI completion dichotomy (i.e., completion of the FEI versus both the ESI and noncompletion of the FEI) using the baseline predictors for that outcome variable. Although the nominal distinction was between FEI completers and all other youths, using FEI versus ESI as one of the variables in the preliminary regression yields a residual that is essentially a comparison between FEI completers and FEI noncompleters and has no association with the other predictors. In each regression analysis, the baseline predictor variables were entered in a single step, followed by the FEI versus ESI group assignment variable, and then the residualized FEI completion variable. Reflective of the primary purpose in our outcome analyses of testing the efficacy of FEI in comparison to ESI, we employed one-sided tests for the group assignment variable and the residualized variable comparing FEI completers and FEI noncompleters (Dembo, Seeberger, et al., 2000).

Predicting Self-Reported Delinquency During the Last Follow-Up Period

General theft offenses. Table 4.8 displays the results of a stepwise regression analysis predicting the youths' self-reported general theft offenses at last interview. The baseline predictors had $R^2 = 0.241$. The R^2 change (.003) associated with the FEI-ESI group assignment variable was quite low and nonsignificant. A low and nonsignificant R^2 change value (.002) was associated with the residualized variable comparing FEI completers and FEI noncompleters. Overall, the predictor variables accounted for 24.6 percent of the variance.

Crimes against persons. The results of the analysis predicting the youths' self-reported crimes against persons at last interview showed the baseline predictors had $R^2 = 0.257$. The R^2 change (.000) associ-

TABLE 4.8. Results of Regression Analyses of Self-Reported Delinquency During the Twelve Months Preceding Last Follow-Up Interview (n = 278)

Variable	R^2 (15 Baseline Characteristics)	R^2 Change: FEI vs. ESI	R^2 Change: FEI Completion	Overall R^2
General theft offenses	.241****	.003	.002	.246****
Crimes against persons	.257****	.000	.008**	.265****
Index crimes	.227****	.000	.003	.230****
Drug sales	.352****	.000	.009**	.361****
Total delinquency	.332****	.000	.009**	.341****

Note: Tests of FEI vs. ESI and FEI completion were one-sided. Tests of R^2 were not directional.
*.10 > p > .05
**p < .05
***p < .01
****p < .001

ated with the FEI-ESI group assignment variable was quite low and nonsignificant. However, a statistically significant R^2 change value (.008) was associated with the residualized variable comparing FEI completers and FEI noncompleters. Compared to FEI noncompleters, FEI completers reported committing fewer crimes against persons. Overall, the predictor variables accounted for 26.5 percent of the variance.

Index crimes. In the analysis predicting the youths' self-reported index crimes at last interview, the baseline predictor variables had $R^2 = 0.227$. The R^2 change (.000) associated with the FEI-ESI group assignment variable was low and nonsignificant. A nonsignificant R^2 change value of .003 was associated with the residualized variable comparing FEI completers and FEI noncompleters. Overall, the predictor variables accounted for 23.0 percent of the variance.

Drug sales. The analysis predicting the youths' self-reported drug sales at last interview found the baseline predictor variables had $R^2 = 0.352$. The R^2 change associated with the FEI-ESI group assignment variable was .000. The R^2 change associated with the residualized variable comparing FEI completers and FEI noncompleters (.009) was significant. Compared to FEI noncompleters, FEI completers reported engaging in fewer drug sales. Overall, the predictor variables accounted for 36.1 percent of the variance.

Total delinquency. Table 4.8 also displays the results of the analysis predicting the youths' self-reported total delinquency at last interview. The baseline predictor variables had $R^2 = 0.332$. In addition, the R^2 change (.000) associated with the FEI-ESI group assignment variable was quite low and nonsignificant. A significant R^2 change value (.009) was associated with the residualized variable comparing FEI completers and FEI noncompleters. Compared to FEI noncompleters, FEI completers reported engaging in less total delinquency. Overall, the predictor variables accounted for 34.1 percent of the variance.

Time and Treatment Group by Time Effects
on the Psychosocial Outcome Measures

Additional regression analyses for each of the outcome measures were performed to determine the effect of length of the follow-up interval and to assess the interaction between the variable reflecting completion of the FEI versus noncompletion and follow-up length. The results of these analyses indicated the following: (1) statistically significant reductions in self-reported general theft crimes, crimes against persons, and total delinquency occurred over time, and (2) the interaction effects of completion of the FEI versus noncompletion and follow-up length were not significant, with one slight exception. For total delinquency, FEI completers had lower rates of reported involvement in total delinquency than FEI noncompleters during the first follow-up and third follow-up years, but the two groups had equal rates of reported involvement in total delinquency during the second follow-up year. Inspection of group means indicated that, with the exception noted above, youths completing the FEI had consistently better outcomes at each time in regard to claimed involvement in crimes against persons, drug sales, and total delinquency.

Summary of Self-Reported Delinquency Findings

Overall, the results of our analyses of self-reported delinquency during the twelve-month and last follow-up periods indicate that youths completing the FEI had significantly lower self-reported rates of crimes against persons, drug sales, and total delinquency than youths not completing the FEI. These results took into account group differences on a wide variety of demographic, psychosocial, offense history, and abuse-neglect history variables. In addition, the findings held up under further study of interaction with time. Although statistically significant, the intervention accounts for under 2 percent of the variation in any dependent variable. Abelson (1985), however, has suggested that the proportion of variation may not be a useful measure of the importance of a predictor.

An alternative explanation for our findings is that youths did better because they were amenable to intervention rather than as the effect of the intervention. However, if this were the case, one would expect that there would be other differences in baseline characteristics, which we did not find. Neither FEI versus ESI youths nor FEI completers versus FEI noncompleters differed significantly on the baseline characteristics (FEI versus ESI, chi-squared test of Wilks' lambda = 14.47, df = 14, p = n.s.; FEI completers versus noncompleters, chi-squared test of Wilks' lambda = 9.76, df = 14, p = n.s.).

These important effects are depicted in Figures 4.6 to 4.8, which display the mean values at last interview for transformed variables for self-reported frequency of crimes against persons (Figure 4.6), drug sales (Figure 4.7), and total delinquency (Figure 4.8). In each case, youths completing the FEI had lower rates of these behaviors than ESI youths or youths not completing the FEI.

The long-term effects of completing the FEI are less robust than the short-term impact of completing the intervention on the youths' self-reported delinquency. Since the intervention was designed to be short term, and no additional services were systematically applied following completion of the FEI, the long-term outcome effects we found were gratifying. We believe the strength of the *sustained effect* of the intervention could have been enhanced by periodic booster sessions designed to support the client youths and families in maintaining their intervention gains.

Our findings on the relationships between completing the FEI and lower self-reported delinquency over time parallel the findings resulting from our analyses of the long-term impact of the FEI on the youths' official record outcomes. Those analyses indicated that youths completing the FEI experienced marginally statistically significant

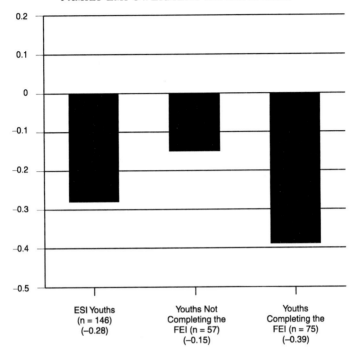

FIGURE 4.6. Adjusted Mean Values of Transformed Frequency of Crimes Against Persons at Last Interview for ESI Youths, Youths Not Completing the FEI, and Youths Completing the FEI

lower rates of new charges and very close to statistically significant lower rates of new arrests than youths not completing the FEI.

The long-term outcome analyses we completed provide evidence of the *sustained effect* of the FEI on delinquency among youths completing the FEI. These findings are particularly important in light of the experience that the salutary effects of intervention programs for high-risk youth are, unfortunately, often short-lived. As noted previously, the Center for the Study and Prevention of Violence (1999) states that the treatment or intervention gains of most programs are lost after participation in the intervention or soon thereafter. The intervention effects we found are consistent with the main hypothesis of this project. Further, as we discuss in Chapter 7, substantial direct cost savings for the justice system can be anticipated from using this intervention.

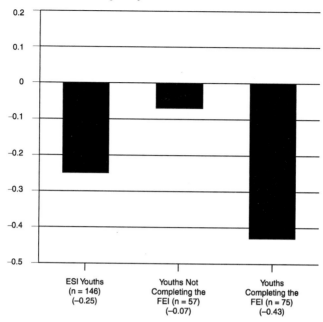

FIGURE 4.7. Adjusted Mean Values of Transformed Frequency of Drug Sales at Last Interview for ESI Youths, Youths Not Completing the FEI, and Youths Completing the FEI

INFLUENCE OF CHANGE IN PROJECT'S CLINICAL LEADERSHIP ON OUTCOMES

The clinical leadership of the project changed in March 1996, at which time the clinical director was replaced by a clinical coordinator and two line supervisors. Hence, a dummy-coded variable was created to reflect whether families entered the project prior to (0) or subsequent to (1) March 1996. This variable was incorporated in additional stepwise regression analyses relating to total number of charges and arrests and to the self-reported delinquency outcome data. These analyses indicated that time of entry into the project did not have an appreciable effect on the results of our analyses of the youths' short- and long-term official record data and self-reported delinquency.

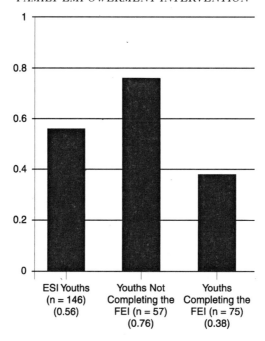

FIGURE 4.8. Adjusted Mean Values of Transformed Total Delinquency at Last Interview for ESI Youths, Youths Not Completing the FEI, and Youths Completing the FEI

Chapter 5

Impact of the Family Empowerment Intervention on Alcohol and Other Drug Use

Drug use among youths remains a major concern nationally. Studies on youths in the general population provide continuing evidence of substantial levels of substance use. The 1999 National Household Survey on Drug Abuse (Substance Abuse and Mental Health Services Administration, 2000) found that 28 percent of youths aged twelve to seventeen reported using an illicit drug in their lifetime (20 percent reported such use in the past year). Further, the 1999 Monitoring the Future survey (Johnston, O'Malley, and Bachman, 1999) found that 28 percent of eighth graders, 46 percent of tenth graders, and 55 percent of twelfth graders reported lifetime use of an illicit drug (20 percent, 36 percent, and 42 percent, respectively, reported illicit drug use in the past year). These estimates are likely to be underestimates because high-risk youths, such as those involved in the juvenile justice system, tend to be underrepresented in these surveys.

Studies of youths entering the juvenile justice system, particularly studies involving urine testing (Dembo, Williams, Berry, et al., 1990; National Institute of Justice, 1999) or hair analysis (Mieczkowski, Newel, and Wright, 1998), have found their rates of drug use to be consistently higher than the rates in national population surveys of youths. For example, recent urine test data from cities participating in the National Institute of Justice's (1999) Arrestee Drug Abuse Monitoring Program (ADAM) indicate high rates of recent drug use among male juvenile arrestees/detainees. (Because of small sample sizes, data on female juvenile arrestees/detainees are not included in the report.) Positive rates for any drug ranged from a low of 40 percent in St. Louis to a high of 69 percent in Phoenix. Marijuana use primarily accounted for these high rates; the median rate positive for this drug was 49 percent in 1998. Cocaine use, which is typically lower than marijuana use among juvenile male arrestees, ranged from 3 to 15 percent at the thirteen ADAM sites testing juvenile arrestees.

Strong statistical correlations have been found between drug use and crime in samples of juveniles entering the criminal justice system (Dembo, Williams, Berry, et al., 1990; Dembo, Pacheco, et al., 1997). Further, Florida has experienced a threefold increase in juvenile drug cases since 1990 (Florida Office of Drug Control, 2000), which has placed additional burdens on already overly stressed juvenile courts and adolescent treatment systems. Relatedly, juvenile drug abusers are also at high risk of being infected by and transmitting the human immunodeficiency virus (HIV) especially through injecting drugs or cocaine-related sexual activity involving multiple partners (Inciardi et al., 1991); and Wish et al. (1992) have identified persons having contact with the justice system as an important HIV/AIDS risk-reduction target group. Drug use has also been found to be associated with other health problems, including other sexually transmitted diseases, teen pregnancies, and infant mortality. For these reasons, legislators and other public policymakers have shown great interest in juvenile drug use and support efforts to reduce adolescent alcohol and other drug use.

Reflective of these concerns, our analyses of the impact of the Family Empowerment Intervention (FEI) on alcohol/other drug use among youths involved in the Youth Support Program (YSP) included both self-report and biological test data to examine short- and long-term use. Paralleling the analyses reported in Chapter 4, and as discussed in more detail in this chapter, the short-term drug use analyses covered the twelve months following the youths' baseline interviews. The long-term drug use analyses covered twelve to thirty-six months following the youths' baseline interviews. The drug use analyses involved 272 youths in the short-term follow-up studies (Time 1), and 278 youths in the long-term outcome analyses, out of 315 eligible youths who entered the project between September 1, 1994, and January 31, 1998. Also, for reasons discussed in Chapter 4, we included a variable in the analyses reflecting whether the youth was a nonserious offender (diversion case) or more serious offender (non-diversion case) and a variable reflecting the interaction of the youth's case type and assignment to the FEI or ESI group on his or her alcohol/other drug use.

SHORT-TERM IMPACT
ON ALCOHOL /OTHER DRUG USE

As discussed in Chapter 3, we adopted a number of questions on drug use from the National Household Survey on Drug Abuse to determine the youths' use of various categories of substances: alcohol, marijuana/hashish in nonblunt form, marijuana in blunt form, inhalants, hallucinogens, cocaine, heroin, and the nonmedical use of barbiturates and other sedatives, tranquilizers, stimulants, and analgesics.

Self-Reported Alcohol Use During Time 1

The survey questions regarding the youths' alcohol use probed their age of first use, recency of use, the number of days used in the past month, and the number of times the youth got very high or drunk on alcohol in the past year. In Chapter 3, we discussed the youths' use of alcohol in the twelve months prior to their baseline interview. Reported frequency of alcohol use for the 272 youths was essentially the same as for the 315 youths discussed in that chapter. For this analysis of alcohol use data, we focused on the youths' responses to the question probing the number of times being very high or drunk on alcohol in the twelve months following random assignment to the FEI or ESI group. As Table 5.1 indicates, 21 percent of the youths reported getting very high or drunk on alcohol twelve or more days per year during Time 1. This rate is similar to the past year rate reported by the youths at the time of their baseline interviews (19 percent).

Self-Reported Illicit-Drug Use During Time 1

Questions concerning the youths' illicit-drug use or nonmedical use of psychotherapeutic drugs probed their age of first use, lifetime frequency of use, and recency of use. In Chapter 3, we discussed the youths' use of illicit drugs prior to their baseline interview (see Table 3.6). In the Time 1 analysis, reported rates of illicit-drug use for

TABLE 5.1. Self-Reported Frequency of Getting Very High or Drunk on Alcohol

Frequency	In Year Before Baseline Interview (%) (n = 272)	During First Follow-Up Period (%) (n = 272)	During 12 Months Prior to Last Interview (%) (n = 278)
None	56	53	48
One or two days	11	11	16
Three to five days	6	10	12
Every other month or so (or six to eleven days)	8	6	6
One to two times a month (or twelve to twenty-four days a year)	6	6	7
Several times a month (or twenty-five to fifty-one days a year)	3	6	5
About one or two days a week	5	6	4
Almost daily (or three to six days a week)	4	2	2
Daily	1	1	2
Total	100	101*	102*

*Total exceeds 100% due to rounding.

the 272 youths (see Table 5.2) were essentially the same as those of the 315 youths represented in Table 3.6.

As shown in Table 5.2, at the time of their first follow-up interview, the youths reported relatively high rates of marijuana/hashish use (including the use of blunts)—28 percent reported using 100 or more times. This compares with 30 percent in the year prior to their baseline interview. Little use of the other categories of drugs probed was claimed. Self-reported use of marijuana/hashish during Time 1 was not corrected for time at risk. This variable was coded as a categorical variable, with each code referring to a range of values. Relatively few youths had a time at risk small enough to increase their scores. Thus, such a refinement in scoring would not have had a substantial effect on the analyses.

TABLE 5.2. Youths' Reported Frequency of Drug Use During the First Follow-Up Period

Drug	Never Used (%)	Used 1 or 2 Times (%)	Used 3 to 5 Times (%)	Used 6 to 10 Times (%)	Used 11 to 49 Times (%)	Used 50 to 99 Times (%)	Used 100 to 199 Times (%)	Used 200 or More Times (%)	Total (n = 271 or 272)
Marijuana/Hashish (including blunts)	36	11	8	3	8	6	7	21	100
Inhalants	95	3	1	2	<1	–	–	–	101
Hallucinogens	85	7	1	3	3	1	–	–	100
Cocaine	87	6	2	1	3	<1	<1	–	99
Heroin	97	1	1	<1	–	–	–	–	99
Nonmedical Use of									
Stimulants	97	2	1	<1	–	–	–	–	100
Sedatives	98	1	1	<1	–	–	–	–	100
Tranquilizers	94	3	1	<1	1	<1	–	–	99
Analgesics	97	2	<1	<1	1	–	–	–	100

117

Hair Testing for Drug Use

Baseline Interview Hair Test Results

In Chapter 3 we reported that as part of their baseline interview, before random assignment to the FEI or ESI group, youths were asked to provide a hair sample for drug testing. The samples were tested for the use of five drugs (marijuana, cocaine, opiates, methamphetamines, and PCP) over the prior ninety days. Results of the youths' baseline hair tests indicated that 44 percent of the youths tested were positive on one or more of the five drugs: 31 percent were positive on one drug (most often marijuana [22 percent], then cocaine [10 percent]), 12 percent were positive on two drugs (most often marijuana and cocaine [10 percent]), and 1 percent were positive on three drugs. Overall, 34 percent of the youths were positive on marijuana and 21 percent were positive on cocaine. Extremely few youths were found positive for PCP, opiates, or methamphetamines. (See Chapter 3 for more information on hair testing for substance use.)

Time 1 Hair Test Results

Hair specimens were collected from 208 youths at the time of their first follow-up (Time 1) interview. No samples were taken from thirty-four youths who were interviewed in long-term secure facilities, nine youths refused to provide a hair sample, and no hair samples were taken from twenty-one youths for other reasons. The test results in the Time 1 period continued to reflect high rates of drug use among the youths. Overall, 56 percent of the youths tested were positive on one or more of the five drugs, 38 percent were positive on one drug (again, most often marijuana [31 percent]), and 17 percent were positive on two drugs (again, most often marijuana and cocaine [16 percent]). Forty-seven percent of the youths were positive on marijuana, and 23 percent were positive on cocaine. Again, extremely few youths had hair tests positive for PCP (none), opiates (1 percent), or methamphetamines (1 percent).

A Preliminary Study of Urine and Hair Testing

We conducted a preliminary study on the ninety-five youths who entered the YSP during its first year and who also completed their first follow-up interview (Time 1). The study compared the youths' self-reports of drug use and the results of the urine and hair tests to determine the relative insight they provided into drug use as measured at their baseline interview (self-reports and hair tests) and at Time 1 (self-reports, urine tests, and hair tests) (Dembo, Shemwell, et al., 1999). At the Time 1 interview, 84 percent of these youths provided a hair sample for testing and 76 percent provided a urine specimen. No hair samples were collected from 8 percent of the youths, and no urine samples were obtained from 13 percent of the youths, because they were in a secure facility (e.g., jail) for a period exceeding the surveillance window of the test (ninety days for hair and thirty days for urine). We encountered few refusals to provide a hair or urine sample (7 percent).

We selected for further analysis the eighty youths who provided a hair sample at their Time 1 follow-up interview. Urine test data were available on sixty-eight (85 percent) of these youths. The collected urine specimens were analyzed using the EMIT process for the presence of six drugs (cannabinoids [THC], cocaine, barbiturates, opiates, PCP, and amphetamines) in line with the guidelines of the American Correctional Association and the Institute for Behavior and Health, Inc. (1991). Psychemedics performed radioimmunoassay RIAH testing of the hair samples for use over the past ninety days of the following substances: cocaine, opiates, PCP, methamphetamines, and marijuana.

The hair test results for marijuana and cocaine at the baseline interview were compared with the youths' self-reported recency of use during the ninety-day period covered by the hair tests. Eighty-seven percent of the youths who tested positive for marijuana reported use in the prior ninety days, and 35 percent of the marijuana-negative youths claimed use in the prior ninety days. In contrast to the high reported use among youths testing positive for marijuana, only one of the fifteen cocaine-positive youths (7 percent) self-reported use of the drug within the past ninety days. Further, only 8 percent of the cocaine-negative youths claimed use during this period of time. This difference in rates of self-reported marijuana and cocaine use may be explained by the fact that cocaine use is less socially acceptable than marijuana use.

Additional analyses compared a composite of the youths' urine test and hair test results for marijuana and cocaine at Time 1 with their self-reported recency of use of each of the two drugs. The results, again, indicated the youths were more willing to admit to the use of marijuana than cocaine. Seventy-one percent of youths who had hair tests positive for marijuana, and 20 percent of youth who had negative hair tests, admitted use in the past three months. In contrast, all eleven youths with a hair test positive for cocaine denied use in the past ninety days, and only one of the youths with negative hair and urine tests reported use in the past ninety days. From this preliminary study we concluded that

1. a large proportion of the youths were marijuana users and a smaller proportion were cocaine users;
2. drug testing indicates much higher rates of cocaine use than self-reports;
3. youths are more willing to report the use of marijuana than cocaine; and
4. hair testing for drug use is a particularly valuable tool for identifying recent drug use and treatment need among arrested youths—particularly cocaine—due to its longer surveillance window than urine testing.

Based on the results of this preliminary study, we decided to use the results of the youths' hair tests as the only biological measure of recent drug use in our various outcome analyses.

Analytic Strategy and Results

As in the self-reported delinquency analyses reported in Chapter 4, the major focus of our short-term analyses was to determine the impact of assignment to the FEI or ESI group on the youths' alcohol and other drug use during Time 1—the one year following their baseline interview. Accordingly, separate stepwise regression analyses, with mean substitution for missing predictors, were performed on the youths' (1) claimed frequency of getting very high or drunk on alcohol during Time 1 and (2) reported frequency of marijuana/hashish use during Time 1; separate stepwise logistic regression analyses were completed predicting the youths' recent (3) marijuana and (4) cocaine use at Time 1 as indicated by their RIAH hair test results.

The frequency of getting very high or drunk on alcohol was coded as 0 = not used; 1 = one or two days in the past twelve months; 2 = three to five days in the past twelve months; 3 = every other month or so (or six to eleven days a year); 4 = one to two times a month (or twelve to twenty-four times a year); 5 = several times a month (or about twenty-five to fifty-one days a year); 6 = about one or two days a week; 7 = almost daily (or three to six days a week); 8 = daily. The frequency of marijuana use was coded as 0 = not used; 1 = one or two times; 2 = three to five times; 3 = six to ten times; 4 = eleven to forty-nine times; 5 = fifty to ninety-nine times; 6 = 100 to 199 times; 7 = 200 or more times. No adjustment was made for time at risk because this seldom changed the frequency category.

Prior to conducting the regression analyses, we completed a principal components analysis on twenty-three of the youths' baseline psychosocial, offense history, and abuse-neglect history variables, similar to the analyses discussed in Chapter 4. Our main interest in completing the stepwise multiple regression and logistic regression analyses was to control for the cumulative effect of various baseline predictor variables before examining the effect of FEI (coded 1) or ESI (coded 0) group assignment. In each analysis, the baseline counterpart of the Time 1 outcome variable being predicted was included among the predictor variables. Thus, the baseline predictor variables were entered in a single step in each stepwise analysis, followed by the FEI or ESI group assignment variable and then the case type by group assignment interaction term. As in the analyses reported in Chapter 4, a one-sided test was employed for the group assignment variable. In the interest of conserving space, the detailed results of these regression analyses are not presented here; they can be found in Dembo, Seeberger, et al. (2000). Our summary reporting of the effects of the youths' baseline predictor variables reflects the primary purpose of this study: to test the efficacy of FEI in comparison to ESI, which served as a less-intensive control intervention. A secondary interest is to ascertain whether there was an interactive effect involving case type by group assignment on the outcome variables.

Since the RIAH test results are dichotomous, separate stepwise logistic regression analyses were performed to identify the factors predicting the youths' recent use of marijuana/hashish and cocaine at their Time 1 interview (Hanushek and Jackson, 1977; Demaris, 1992;

Menard, 1995). Twenty-one cases were missing marijuana hair test results for their baseline interview (most often due to insufficient quantity for testing). The missing data were replaced by the mean of this variable to retain as many cases as possible in the analyses.

Predicting Self-Reported Frequency
of Getting Very High/Drunk on Alcohol
During Time 1

Table 5.3 shows the results of the stepwise regression analysis predicting the youths' coded frequency of getting very high or drunk on alcohol during the first follow-up period. The baseline predictor variables, including the youths' baseline reported frequency of getting very high or drunk on alcohol, had $R^2 = 0.285$. The R^2 change value (.017) associated with the FEI-ESI group assignment variable was statistically significant ($F = 6.16$; df = 1,255; $p < .007$—one-sided). After adjusting for baseline variables, youths receiving FEI services averaged 1.32 on the coded alcohol frequency variable compared to 1.80 for youths receiving ESI services. The R^2 change (.003) associated with the case type by group assignment interaction term was low

TABLE 5.3. Results of Regression Analyses Involving Self-Reported Alcohol and Marijuana Use During First Follow-Up Period (n = 272)

Variable	R^2 (15 Baseline Characteristics)	R^2 Change FEI vs. ESI	R^2 Change: Case Type × Group Assignment	Overall R^2
Coded frequency of getting very high/ drunk on alcohol	.285****	.017***	.003	.305****
Coded frequency of marijuana use	.439****	.011**	.000	.450****

Note: Group-assignment significance levels are for a one-sided test. All other significance levels are not directional.
*.10 > p > .05
**p < .05
***p < .01
****p < .001

and nonsignificant. Overall, the predictor variables accounted for 30.5 percent of the variance.

Figure 5.1 shows the mean values for the youths' coded frequency of getting very high or drunk on alcohol, which have been adjusted for their baseline demographic and psychosocial characteristics, delinquency and dependency referral history, and self-reported abuse experiences. Youths not completing the FEI averaged 1.75 compared to 1.00 for youths who completed the FEI. Youths not completing the FEI were similar to the ESI youths (1.80).

Predicting Self-Reported Frequency of Marijuana/Hashish Use During Time 1

Table 5.3 also displays the results of a stepwise regression analysis predicting the youths' reported frequency of marijuana/hashish use

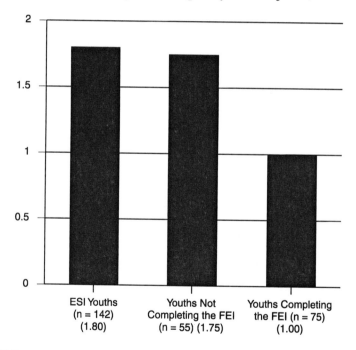

FIGURE 5.1. Adjusted Mean Values of Self-Reported Coded Frequency of Getting Very High or Drunk on Alcohol During the Follow-Up Period for ESI Youths, Youths Not Completing the FEI, and Youths Completing the FEI

during Time 1. The R^2 of the baseline predictor variables, including the youths' lifetime frequency of marijuana/hashish use reported at the baseline interview, was 0.439. In addition, the R^2 change reflecting FEI or ESI group assignment (.011) was statistically significant ($F = 4.91$; df = 1,255; $p = .014$—one-sided). Youths receiving FEI services averaged 2.57 on the coded marijuana frequency variable compared to 3.09 for youths receiving ESI services. The case type by group assignment interaction was low and nonsignificant (R^2 change = .000). Overall, the predictor variables accounted for 45 percent of the variance.

Figure 5.2 displays the mean values for the youths' coded marijuana use, which have been adjusted for their baseline demographic and psychosocial characteristics, delinquency and dependency referral history, and self-reported abuse experiences. Youths not completing the FEI averaged 3.00 on the coded marijuana frequency variable compared to 2.25 for youths completing the FEI. Youths not completing the FEI were similar to the ESI youths (3.09).

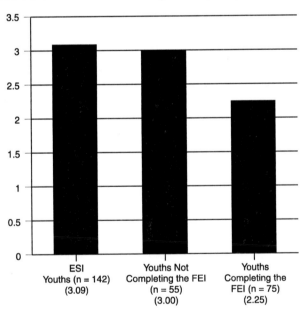

FIGURE 5.2. Adjusted Mean Values of Self-Reported Coded Frequency of Marijuana Use During the Follow-Up Period for ESI Youths, Youths Not Completing the FEI, and Youths Completing the FEI

Predicting Recent Marijuana Use at Time 1

The results of the stepwise logistic regression analysis predicting marijuana use at Time 1 for the 174 youths with RIAH test results for this drug are presented in Table 5.4. The baseline predictors were significantly associated with follow-up marijuana use. The chi-square change relating to FEI or ESI group assignment was also statistically significant. After adjusting for baseline variables, compared to youths receiving ESI services, youths receiving FEI services had a significantly lower rate of positive hair tests for marijuana. No significant case type by group assignment effect was found in regard to the youths' Time 1 marijuana test results.

Figure 5.3 displays the percentage of youths who had positive hair tests for marijuana at their Time 1 interview. As can be seen, 64 percent of ESI youths and 64 percent of youths not completing the FEI were marijuana positive compared to 48 percent of youths completing the FEI.

Predicting Recent Cocaine Use at Time 1

A stepwise logistic regression analysis was completed to identify the predictors of the youths' RIAH test results for cocaine at their Time 1 interview. Table 5.4 also presents these results. The baseline

TABLE 5.4. Results of Logistic Regression Analyses of Hair Test Results for Marijuana and Cocaine Use During First Follow-Up Interview

Variable	Chi-Square (15 Baseline Characteristics)	Chi-Square Change: FEI vs. ESI	Chi-Square Change: Case Type × Group Assignment
Hair test results for marijuana (n = 174)	56.37****	3.65**	2.15
Hair test results for cocaine (n = 208)	82.80****	0.03	4.12**

Note: Group-assignment significance levels are for a one-sided test. All other significance levels are not directional.

*.10 > p > .05
**p < .05
***p < .01
****p <.001

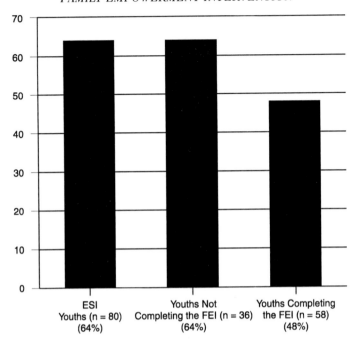

FIGURE 5.3. Hair Test Results for Marijuana at Follow-Up Interview for ESI Youths, Youths Not Completing the FEI, and Youths Completing the FEI

predictors were significantly associated with follow-up cocaine use, but FEI or ESI group assignment was not significantly related to being cocaine positive at first follow-up. However, a statistically significant case type by group assignment interaction effect was found. Compared to ESI services, FEI services were beneficial (i.e., a lower rate of positive hair tests for cocaine) among diversion cases, but among nondiversion cases the result was in the opposite direction.

Does Completion of the FEI Make a Difference in Short-Term Outcome?

As noted in Chapter 4, 58 percent of 130 youths and families receiving FEI services completed the intervention, but 42 percent did not. A discriminant analysis comparing the FEI cases that did and did not complete the intervention on the fourteen baseline variables revealed no statistically significant differences between the two groups on any of the comparison variables. Since the sample sizes were smaller, and to simplify presentation of results, these two subgroups of FEI cases were compared using one-sided *t* tests or chi-square tests. These differences did not adjust for association with baseline characteristics. Table 5.5 presents these results and the ESI group results for comparison.

A statistically significant difference was found between youths not completing the FEI and youths completing the FEI on frequency of getting very high or drunk on alcohol during Time 1. Marginally statistically significant differences were found for two other drug outcome variables (self-reported frequency of marijuana use during Time 1 and hair test results for marijuana at Time 1). In each case, youths completing the FEI had lower rates of drug use (measured by self-reports and hair test results) than youths not completing the FEI.

Comparison of youths who did and did not complete the FEI shows clearly that its success was due to those youths who completed the intervention. Youths who did not complete the FEI did not differ from ESI youths. This supports the efficacy of the intervention. An alternative explanation is that youths did better because they were amenable to intervention, rather than as the effect of the intervention. However, if this were the case, one would expect that there would be other differences in baseline characteristics, which we did not find.

LONG-TERM IMPACT ON ALCOHOL/OTHER DRUG USE

Self-Reported Alcohol Use at Last Interview

Table 5.1 shows that 19 percent of the youths reported they had gotten very high or drunk on alcohol twelve or more days in the twelve months preceding their baseline interview. Since the baseline interview results for the 278 youths involved in the long-term follow-up analyses were almost identical to those of the 272 youths at baseline, they are not presented separately. Table 5.1 also indicates that 20 percent of the 278 youths involved in the long-term outcome analyses reported getting very high or drunk on alcohol twelve or more days during the year preceding their last follow-up interview. This rate is similar to the rate reported by them at the time of their baseline interviews.

TABLE 5.5. Comparison of Drug Use Outcome Variables Across ESI Youths, Youths Not Completing the FEI, and Youths Completing the FEI

Comparison Variable	ESI Youths (n = 142)	Youths Not Completing the FEI (n = 55)	Youths Completing the FEI (n = 75)	t Value of Not Completing vs. Completing
Self-reported coded frequency of getting very high/drunk on alcohol during the follow-up period	1.80	1.75	1.00	2.04** (df = 90.80)
Marijuana use during the follow-up period	3.09	3.00	2.25	1.52* (df = 106.38)

	ESI Youths (n = 142)	Youths Not Completing the FEI (n = 55)	Youths Completing the FEI (n = 75)	X² Value of Not Completing vs. Completing
Hair test positive for Marijuana at follow-up interview	64% (n = 80)	64% (n = 36)	48% (n = 58)	2.18* (df = 1)
Cocaine at follow-up interview	24% (n = 103)	29% (n = 41)	20% (n = 64)	1.10 (df = 1)

Note: t test or chi-square significance levels are one-sided.
*.10 > *p* > .05
** *p* < .05
*** *p* < .01
**** *p* < .001

128

Self-Reported Illicit-Drug Use at Last Interview

Table 5.6 presents the self-reported drug use of the 278 youths, both lifetime prior to baseline interview and during the year preceding their last interview. Drugs with very low reported frequencies of use have been excluded from the table. In terms of reported lifetime frequency of use prior to baseline interview, over half (55 percent) of the youths used marijuana in nonblunt form, and almost as many (50 percent) in blunt form. The reported use of hallucinogens (14 percent) and cocaine (13 percent) was at much lower rates. No other drug was used by more than 10 percent of the youths. Seventeen percent of the youths claimed to have used marijuana/hashish in nonblunt form, and 11 percent marijuana in blunt form, 100 or more times in their lives prior to their baseline interview. Since the reported lifetime frequency of marijuana/hashish use in nonblunt form and in blunt form was strongly associated ($r = .693$, $n = 278$, $p < .001$), a composite index of the youths' use of marijuana/hashish was created, summing standardized coded scores for these two variables, for use in subsequent analyses. The lifetime drug use prevalence rates shown in Table 5.6 are higher than those reported by the youths aged twelve to seventeen who were interviewed in the 1996 National Household Survey on Drug Abuse (NHSDA; Substance Abuse and Mental Health Services Administration, 1997) (given in parentheses): marijuana/hashish—55 percent (versus 17 percent in the NHSDA sample), hallucinogens—14 percent (versus 6 percent), and cocaine—13 percent (versus 2 percent).

At the time of their last follow-up interview, the youths also reported relatively high rates of marijuana/hashish use (including the use of blunts) in the past year—31 percent reported use 100 or more times. Again, little use of the other categories of drugs probed was reported (see Table 5.6). Self-reported use of marijuana/hashish during the follow-up period was not corrected for time at risk. This variable was coded as a categorical variable, with each code referring to a range of values. Relatively few youths had a time at risk small enough to increase their scores if they were in intermediate categories. Thus, such a refinement in scoring would not have had an appreciable effect on the analyses.

TABLE 5.6. Youths' Reported Frequency of Drug Use

Drug	Never Used (%)	Used 1 to 2 Times (%)	Used 3 to 5 Times (%)	Used 6 to 10 Times (%)	Used 11 to 49 Times (%)	Used 50 to 99 Times (%)	Used 100 to 199 Times (%)	Used 200+ Times (%)	Total (n = 277 or 278) (%)
Lifetime prior to baseline interview									
Marijuana/hashish (nonblunt)	45	8	5	5	15	4	4	13	99
Blunts	50	12	7	7	9	4	3	8	100
Hallucinogens	86	6	2	2	3	1	—	—	100
Cocaine	87	6	1	1	2	1	<1	<1	98
Year preceding last interview									
Marijuana/hashish (including blunts)	39	8	5	5	6	5	9	22	99
Hallucinogens	86	8	1	2	2	<1	—	<1	99
Cocaine	87	4	5	1	2	<1	—	1	100

Hair Testing for Drug Use at Last Interview

Again, the results of assays of the youths' hair samples were an important component of our outcome analyses. Table 5.7 presents the drug test results for the youths for whom we had hair samples to analyze at the time of their baseline and last follow-up interviews. There was a dramatic increase in the percentage of youths found to be drug positive: 71 percent at the last follow-up interview compared to 44 percent at the baseline interview. Most of this change was a result of a dramatic increase in the rate of positives for marijuana (from 38 percent at baseline to 66 percent at last follow-up interview). Most of the youths with missing hair samples were interviewed in long-term secure facilities; few youths refused to provide a hair sample.

Analytic Strategy and Results

As in the self-reported delinquency analyses reported in Chapter 4, the major focus of these analyses is to determine the impact of assignment to the FEI or ESI group on the youths' alcohol or other drug use as measured during their last follow-up interview (Dembo, See-

TABLE 5.7. Hair Test Results (RIAH)

Frequency	At Baseline Interview		Last Interview	
	n	%	n	%
No drug positives	147	56	80	29
Positive for				
Marijuana	90	38[a]	141	66[b]
Cocaine	59	22	64	27
Opiates	5	2	5	2
Methamphetamines	1	<1	9	4
PCP	0	–	0	–
Number of youths providing hair samples	264		235	

[a] Based on 234 samples tested for all five drugs. Excludes thirty samples of hair that were insufficient to test for marijuana.
[b] Based on 213 samples tested for all five drugs. Excludes twenty-two samples of hair that were insufficient to test for marijuana.

berger, et al., 2000). Accordingly, we performed separate stepwise regression analyses, with mean substitution for missing predictors, on the youths' (1) claimed frequency of getting very high or drunk on alcohol during the year preceding the last follow-up interview and (2) reported frequency of marijuana/hashish use during the year prior to the last follow-up interview; separate stepwise logistic regression analyses were completed predicting the youths' recent (3) marijuana and (4) cocaine use at the last follow-up interview, as indicated by their RIAH hair test results.

As we did for the short-term analyses, before conducting the regression analyses, we completed a principal components analysis on twenty-three of the youths' baseline psychosocial, offense history, and abuse-neglect history variables. This analysis identified eight principal components with eigenvalues greater than 1.0 among the twenty-three predictor variables, and they accounted for 58 percent of the variance. Further, the communalities of all variables were .36 to .73, except .29 for RIAH drug test results for marijuana at the baseline interview. These clusters were varimax rotated for factor clarity. Regression factor scores (Kim and Mueller, 1978) were derived for these eight varimax-rotated factors.

Since previous analyses indicated the importance of graduation from the FEI on outcome, we included a residualized variable reflecting graduation from the FEI in our analyses (see Chapter 4 for a detailed discussion). Our interests in completing the multiple regression and logistic regression analyses were to control for the cumulative effect of various baseline predictor variables, including the varimax-rotated factors and the youths' demographic characteristics, before examining the effect on outcome of (1) FEI (coded 1) or ESI (coded 0) group assignment, and (2) the residualized variable reflecting completion of the FEI. In each regression or logistic regression analysis, the baseline predictor variables plus the baseline counterpart of the specific outcome measure being studied were entered in a single step, followed by the FEI or ESI group assignment variable and then the residualized FEI completion variable. Reflective of the primary purpose in our outcome analyses, to test the efficacy of FEI in comparison to ESI, we employed one-sided tests for the group assignment variable and the residualized variable comparing FEI completers and FEI noncompleters.

Predicting Reported Frequency of Getting Very High/Drunk
on Alcohol in Year Prior to Last Interview

Table 5.8 shows the results of the stepwise regression analysis predicting the youths' reported frequency of getting very high or drunk on alcohol during the year prior to their last interview. The baseline predictor variables, including the youths' baseline reported frequency of getting very high or drunk on alcohol, had $R^2 = .213$. The R^2 change value (.002) associated with the FEI-ESI group assignment variable was not statistically significant. However, the R^2 change associated with the residualized variable comparing FEI completers and FEI noncompleters (.013) was statistically significant. Compared to youths not completing the FEI, FEI completers reported getting very high or drunk on alcohol less often. Overall, the predictor variables accounted for 22.8 percent of the variance.

Figure 5.4 presents the mean values for the youths' reported getting very high/drunk on alcohol, which have been adjusted for their baseline demographic, psychosocial, delinquency and dependency referral history, and their self-reported abuse experiences. The ESI youths, youths not completing the FEI, and youths completing the

TABLE 5.8. Results of Regression Analyses Involving Self-Reported Alcohol and Marijuana Use During Year Preceding Last Follow-Up Interview (n = 278)

Variable	R^2 (15 Baseline Characteristics)	R^2 Change FEI vs. ESI	R^2 Change: Residualized FEI Completion Variable	Overall R^2
Coded frequency of getting very high/ drunk on alcohol	.213****	.002	.013***	.228****
Coded frequency of marijuana use	.304****	.001	.003	.308****

Note: Group-assignment significance levels are for a one-sided test. All other significance levels are not directional.
*.10 > *p* > .05
**p* < .05
***p* < .01
****p* <.001

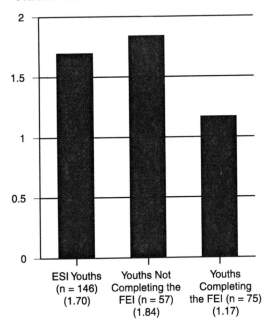

FIGURE 5.4. Adjusted Mean Values of Reported Frequency of Getting Very High or Drunk on Alcohol at Last Interview for ESI Youths, Youths Not Completing the FEI, and Youths Completing the FEI

FEI are represented in the figure. As can be seen, ESI youths, on average, reported a categorical frequency of getting very high or drunk on alcohol of 1.70 compared to 1.84 for youths not completing the FEI, and 1.17 for youths completing the FEI.

Predicting Self-Reported Frequency of Marijuana/Hashish
Use in Year Prior to Last Interview

Table 5.8 also displays the results of a stepwise regression analysis predicting the youths' reported frequency of marijuana/hashish use during the year prior to their last follow-up interview. The R^2 of the baseline predictor variables, including the youths' lifetime frequency of marijuana/hashish use reported at baseline interview, was .304. The R^2 change reflecting FEI or ESI group assignment (.001) was not statistically significant. The residualized variable comparing FEI completers and FEI noncompleters increased R^2 by .003, which was nonsignificant. Overall, the predictor variables accounted for 30.8 percent of the variance.

*Predicting Recent Use of Marijuana/Hashish
and Cocaine at Last Follow-Up Interview
As Determined by RIAH Test Results*

Predicting marijuana use. The results of the stepwise logistic regression analysis predicting marijuana use at the last interview for the 213 youths with RIAH test results for this drug are presented in Table 5.9. The baseline predictors were significantly associated with follow-up marijuana use. The chi-square change relating to FEI or ESI group assignment (1.60) was not statistically significant. The chi-square change associated with the residualized variable comparing FEI completers and FEI noncompleters (0.10) also was nonsignificant.

Predicting cocaine use. A stepwise logistic regression analysis was also completed to identify the predictors of the youths' RIAH test results for cocaine at last observation. The results of this analysis,

TABLE 5.9. Results of Logistic Regression Analyses of Hair Test Results for Marijuana and Cocaine Use at Last Follow-Up Interview

Variable	Model Chi-Square (Improvement Over Null Model)		
	Chi-Square (15 Baseline Characteristics)	Chi-Square Change: FEI vs. ESI	Chi-Square Change: Case Type × Group Assignment
Hair test results for marijuana (n = 213)	49.10****	1.60	0.10
Hair test results for cocaine (n = 235)	55.02****	0.01	0.10

Note: Group-assignment significance levels are for a one-sided test. All other significance levels are not directional.
*.10 > *p* > .05
**p* < .05
***p* < .01
****p* <.001

shown in Table 5.9, indicate that the youths' baseline predictors were significantly associated with cocaine use at the last interview. The low chi-square change associated with FEI or ESI group assignment (0.01) indicated group assignment was not significantly related to this outcome variable. Further, the chi-square change associated with the residualized variable comparing FEI completers and FEI non-completers (0.10) was not significant.

Time and Treatment Group by Time Effects
on the Drug Use Outcome Measures

Additional analyses were performed to determine the effect of length of follow-up time, and to assess separately the interaction between the variable reflecting completion of the FEI versus non-completion and follow-up length, on the youths' reported getting very high/drunk on alcohol. The results of these analyses indicated that the better outcomes of youths completing the FEI in regard to reported frequency of getting very high or drunk on alcohol did not vary substantially with follow-up length.

Summary of Findings from the Outcome Analyses

The results of our short-term analyses provide strong, consistent evidence in support of the efficacy of the FEI. Youths receiving FEI services had statistically significant lower drug use than youths receiving the ESI on three of the four variables tested (getting very high/drunk on alcohol, reported marijuana use, and hair test results for marijuana). These results took into account group differences on a wide variety of demographic, psychosocial, offense history, and abuse-neglect history variables. The findings support the key hypothesis informing this study and indicate the usefulness of this intervention. There was also a significant, hypothesis-consistent effect of completing the FEI compared to not completing the FEI on coded frequency of getting very high/drunk on alcohol, and marginally significant effects on self-reported coded frequency of marijuana use and hair test results for marijuana.

Although statistically significant, the intervention accounts for less than 2 percent of the variation in any dependent variable. Abelson (1985), however, has suggested that the proportion of variation may not be a useful measure of the importance of a predictor. For example, for both the coded alcohol and marijuana variables, a change of one point on the scale increases the rate of use by doubling it or more. Thus, the effect of a difference in group means of half a point is considerable.

Our long-term analyses indicate that youths completing the FEI continued to have significantly lower reported rates of getting very high or drunk on alcohol than youths not completing the FEI. As in the short-term analyses, these results took into account group differences on a wide variety of demographic, psychosocial, offense history, and abuse-neglect history variables. In addition, this finding held up under further study of interaction with length of time to follow-up. Again, an alternative explanation for our findings is that youths did better because they were amenable to intervention rather than as the effect of the intervention, but we did not find other differences in baseline characteristics to support that explanation (see Chapter 4 for reported results).

Similar to the findings reported in Chapter 4 relating to delinquency/crime, the long-term effects of the FEI are less robust than the twelve-month impact of the intervention on the youths' self-reported getting very high/drunk on alcohol. This is consistent with the short-term design of the intervention; no additional services were systematically provided following completion of the FEI. At the same time, the long-term effect of the FEI completion on the adverse use of alcohol is gratifying; the results provide additional evidence of the sustained effect of the FEI.

INFLUENCE OF CHANGE IN PROJECT'S CLINICAL LEADERSHIP ON OUTCOMES

Additional analyses were completed to determine if there were any effects of the change in clinical leadership after March 1996 on the youths' reported frequencies of getting very high/drunk on alcohol, their marijuana use, and their positive hair tests for marijuana or cocaine as measured at their follow-up interview. The results indicated that time of entry into the project did not have an appreciable effect on the above-reported results.

Chapter 6

Impact of the Family Empowerment Intervention on Emotional/Psychological Functioning

The emotional/psychological problems experienced by youths entering the juvenile justice system have been a growing concern. First, it is increasingly recognized that many youths entering the justice system have experienced physical abuse or sexual abuse/exploitation; female youths experience these traumatic events at higher rates than males (Dembo, Williams, and Schmeidler, 1998; Dembo, Pacheco, et al., 1998). Second, many juvenile offenders are experiencing other emotional/psychological problems, such as depression, that inhibit their wholesome functioning and development (Winters, 1998). Third, there is increased awareness of the prevalence of the co-occurring disorders of mental health problems and substance abuse problems among high-risk youths, such as juveniles involved with the justice system (American Academy of Child and Adolescent Psychiatry, 1998; Weinberg et al., 1998). Many of these youths' difficulties can be traced to the fact that family alcohol/other drug use, mental health problems, or criminal behavior existed when the youths were very young (Dembo et al., 1992; Dembo, Wothke, Seeberger, et al., 2000).

An increasing number of cross-sectional (Lewis et al., 1979; Dembo et al., 1989) and longitudinal (Widom, 1989a,b, 1991, 1995; Dembo et al., 1992; Dembo, Wothke, Seeberger, et al., 2000) studies have documented that abused children are at high risk of adverse developmental outcomes. The results of longitudinal studies have provided greater confidence in the connections between these experiences. Abused youths often grow up in troubled families (e.g., alcohol/other drug abuse or mental health problems, violence between family members, and/or involvement with the criminal justice system) (Miller et al., 1987; Lewis et al., 1989). Such factors place these youths at considerable risk for future drug use and delinquency/crime.

In light of these significant concerns, part of our analyses focused on the short- and long-term impact of the Family Empowerment Intervention (FEI) on the youths emotional/psychological functioning. Consistent with the analyses reported in Chapters 4 and 5, and as discussed in more detail below, the short-term emotional/psychological analyses (272 youths) covered the twelve months following the youths' baseline interviews. The long-term analyses (278 youths) covered twelve to thirty-six months following the youths' baseline interviews. Again, we included a variable in the analyses reflecting whether the youth was a nonserious offender (diversion case) or more serious offender (nondiversion case), and we created a variable reflecting the interaction of the youth's case type and assignment to the FEI or ESI group.

SHORT-TERM IMPACT ON EMOTIONAL / PSYCHOLOGICAL FUNCTIONING

Measure of Emotional/Psychological Functioning

The Symptom Check List-90-Revised (SCL-90-R; Derogatis, 1983) was used to assess the youths' emotional/psychological functioning. The youths' replies to the items yielded T scores on nine symptom dimensions:

1. *Somatization:* distress arising from perceptions of bodily dysfunction
2. *Obsessive-compulsive:* symptoms that are closely identified with the standard clinical syndrome of the same name
3. *Interpersonal sensitivity:* feelings of personal inadequacy and inferiority, particularly in comparisons with others
4. *Depression:* a broad range of manifestations of clinical depression
5. *Anxiety:* a set of symptoms and signs that are associated clinically with high levels of manifest anxiety
6. *Hostility:* thoughts, feelings, or actions that are characteristic of the negative affect state of anger

7. *Phobic anxiety:* persistent fear of a specific person, place, object, or situation, characterized as irrational and disproportionate to the stimulus, leading to avoidance or escape behavior
8. *Paranoid ideation:* a disoriented mode of thinking
9. *Psychoticism:* a range of items tapping functioning from mild interpersonal alienation to dramatic evidence of psychosis.

The SCL-90-R has a long developmental history, has very good psychometric properties, and is widely used in clinical settings. It is easily administered (average test time is twelve to fifteen minutes) and interpreted (Derogatis, 1983).

Emotional/Psychological Functioning at Baseline Interview

The *T* score means for the nine SCL-90-R scales at the baseline interview are given in Table 6.1. Comparison of the average *T* score for the nine scales against the mean of 50 and standard deviation of 10 in the standardizing population indicated that the *T* scores for all nine scales were significantly lower than the scores for the normed population (adolescent nonpatients), with $p < .001$ for all nine scales. This low rate of reported problems may be analogous to the low rates of reporting cocaine use compared to marijuana use, discussed in Chapter 5. That was attributed to the stigmatizing nature of cocaine use which might also apply to emotional/psychological problems.

Principal components analysis was completed on the SCL-90-R *T* scores for the nine scale data at each interview wave. Table 6.1 shows the loadings of the single principal component with an eigenvalue greater than 1 at baseline and follow-up analyses. The loadings of the scales on the principal components were similar over time; for each principal component each of the scales loaded highly and positively. Separate regression factor scores (Kim and Mueller, 1978) were created to summarize these data for each principal component. Higher scores indicate more emotional/psychological problems.

Emotional/Psychological Functioning at Time 1 Follow-Up Interview

The *T* score means of the nine SCL-90-R scales at the youths' first follow-up interview (Time 1) are also presented in Table 6.1. These

TABLE 6.1. *T* Score Means for the Nine SCL-90-R Scales and Their Loading on the Main Principal Components, Baseline to Time 3

Scale	Baseline Interview (n = 272)		Time 1 Follow-Up (n = 272)		Time 2 Follow-Up (n = 159)		Time 3 Follow-Up (n = 89)	
	T Score Mean	Loading*	T Score Mean	Loading*	T Score Mean	Loading*	T Score Mean	Loading*
Somatization	45.2	80	44.4	75	44.2	67	45.6	72
Obsessive-compulsive	44.2	88	43.1	87	42.6	86	45.7	90
Interpersonal sensitivity	41.2	91	40.7	88	40.2	90	43.7	94
Depression	44.2	91	43.0	88	42.7	86	44.3	93
Anxiety	44.8	90	42.2	87	41.9	85	44.0	88
Hostility	46.0	80	45.2	76	44.1	78	46.7	85
Phobic anxiety	46.9	76	46.1	79	45.5	77	47.1	80
Paranoid ideation	45.7	87	45.0	86	44.2	89	46.5	88
Psychoticism	44.5	89	43.1	86	43.7	88	45.8	83
Eigenvalue		6.64		6.34		6.24		6.7
Percent of variance		73.8		70.5		69.3		74.5

*Decimal points omitted.

142

mean T scores were all lower than the baseline interview SCL-90-R findings, but only anxiety and psychoticism were statistically significant ($p < .05$). A comparison of the average T scores for the nine scales measured at Time 1 against the standardizing population again indicated that the T score for each of the nine scales was significantly lower than the score for the normed population of adolescent nonpatients, with $p < .001$ for all nine scales.

Analytic Strategy and Results

The analytic strategy discussed in Chapters 4 and 5 was used to assess the impact of assignment to the FEI or ESI group on the youths' emotional/psychological functioning during Time 1. Separate stepwise regression analyses, with mean substitution for missing predictors, were performed on the summary measure scores of the youths' emotional/psychological functioning at Time 1. As discussed in Chapter 4, a principal components analysis was completed on the youths twenty-three baseline psychosocial, offense history, and abuse-neglect history variables. Regression factor scores (Kim and Mueller, 1978) of these eight varimax-rotated principal components, the youths' demographic characteristics (age, race, gender, ethnicity, and living situation), case type, group assignment, and case type by group assignment, and the baseline emotional/psychological functioning factor score were included as predictor variables in the regression analysis. The baseline predictor variables were entered in a single step in the stepwise analysis, followed by the FEI or ESI group assignment variable, and then the case type by group assignment interaction term.

Predicting Emotional/Psychological Functioning at Time 1 Follow-Up Interview

In the stepwise regression analysis predicting the youth's emotional/psychological functioning at the Time 1 follow-up interview, the baseline predictors had $R^2 = 0.217$ (F = 4.72; df = 15,256; $p < .001$). The R^2 change for the variable reflecting ESI or FEI group assignment (.2002) was nonsignificant. The interaction of case type and group increased R^2 by .004, but was nonsignificant. Overall, predictor variables accounted for 22.3 percent of the variance ($F = 4.27$; $df = 17,254$; $p < .001$).

Did Completion of the FEI Make a Difference in Outcome?

As noted in Chapters 4 and 5, 58 percent of 130 youths and families receiving FEI services completed the intervention, but 42 percent did not. Discriminant analysis comparing the FEI cases that did and did not complete the intervention on baseline variables found no statistically significant overall or individual differences between the two groups. Accordingly, these two subgroups of FEI cases were compared on their Time 1 SCL-90-R summary measure scores using a one-sided t test, without adjusting for association with baseline characteristics. Youths completing the FEI averaged .04 on the factor compared to −.02 for youths not completing the FEI. Youths receiving ESI services averaged −.01.

We also repeated these analyses separately for male and female youths. The results indicated no significant differences in emotional/ psychological functioning as measured by the SCL-90-R between FEI and ESI youths and between youths completing and not completing the FEI.

LONG-TERM IMPACT ON EMOTIONAL/ PSYCHOLOGICAL FUNCTIONING

Emotional/Psychological Functioning at Times 2 and 3 Follow-Up Interviews

The T score means for the nine SCL-90-R scales at Times 2 and 3 are also presented in Table 6.1. Comparison of the average T scores for the nine scales against the mean of 50 and standard deviation of 10 in the standardizing population indicates that the T scores for all nine scales are significantly lower than the scores for the normed population (adolescent nonpatients) at $p < .001$ for all scales at Time 2 and $p < .01$ for all scales at Time 3. Since the baseline interview results for the 278 youths involved in the long-term follow-up analyses were almost identical to those for the 272 youths in the short-term analysis, they are not included in the table.

Analytic Strategy and Results

As in the analyses reported in Chapters 4 and 5, the major focus of our analyses here was to determine the impact of assignment to the FEI or ESI group on the youths' emotional/psychological functioning as measured during their last follow-up interview (Dembo, Seeberger, et al., 2000). Hence, a stepwise regression analysis, with mean substitution for missing predictors, was completed on the youths' emotional/psychological functioning as measured at the last follow-up interview. As discussed in Chapter 4, a principal components analysis was completed on twenty-three of the youths' baseline psychosocial, offense history, and abuse-neglect history variables. Since previous analyses reported in Chapters 4 and 5 indicated the importance of graduation from the FEI for outcome, we included a residualized variable reflecting graduation from the FEI in this analysis. The youths' baseline demographic characteristics, case type, regression factor scores on the eight varimax principal components, together with their baseline emotional/psychological functioning factor scores, were entered in a single step; these variables were followed by the FEI or ESI group assignment variable and then the residualized variable reflecting completion of the FEI. In line with our wish to test the efficacy of FEI in comparison to ESI, we employed one-sided tests for the group assignment variable and the residualized variable comparing FEI completers and FEI noncompleters.

Predicting Emotional/Psychological Functioning at Last Follow-Up Interview

In the stepwise regression analyses predicting the youths' emotional/psychological functioning at the last follow-up interview, the various baseline predictor variables had $R^2 = 0.185$ (F = 3.95; df = 15,262; $p < .001$). In contrast, the R^2 change for the variable reflecting ESI or FEI group assignment (.000) was nonsignificant. The residualized variable comparing FEI completers and FEI noncompleters increased R^2 by .004, but this was nonsignificant. Overall, predictor variables accounted for 18.9 percent of the variance ($F = 3.56$; df = 17,260; $p < .001$).

We also repeated this analysis for male and female youths separately. The results indicated that the scores for male and female youths completing the FEI and those not completing the FEI did not differ significantly from one another, or from the scores of ESI youths.

Satisfaction with Family

A second, and equally important, area of emotional/psychological functioning concerns the impact of the FEI on changes in the youths' felt satisfaction with their families and their communication with parents. We used, with permission, the family satisfaction questions developed by Olson and Wilson (1982) to probe the youths' satisfaction with various aspects of their relationship with their families. Study of changes in project youths' reported satisfaction with the family over time is an important new area of focus in our examination of the impact of the FEI. Until this point, our analyses had looked for reductions in problem behavior that might be related to participation in the FEI. Family satisfaction addresses an important area of positive change—improvements in the quality of family life. (Our study of changes in communication with parents/guardians is a second such area.)

Olson and Wilson's (1982) original measure included fourteen items. Each item was answered on a five-point scale: 1 = dissatisfied, 2 = somewhat dissatisfied, 3 = generally satisfied, 4 = very satisfied, 5 = extremely satisfied. However, two of the items reflected a two-parent household (parents making decisions and mother and father arguing). As indicated in Chapter 3, most youths in the YSP did not live in two-parent households, and they did not answer these questions. Accordingly, these two questions were excluded in our analyses. Further, because the youths' living circumstances changed significantly over time, the baseline interview and Time 1 follow-up interview information on satisfaction with family was studied. There were 248 youths for whom complete family satisfaction information was available for this time period. The 248 youths tended to be younger and more often African American than the sixty-seven youths for whom we lacked complete baseline and Time 1 family satisfaction data (mean age 14.5 years versus 15.0 years [$t = -2.15$, df = 313, $p < .05$], African American 42 percent versus 27 percent [chi-square = 5.31, df = 1, $p < .05$], respectively). No significant differences were found in regard to ethnicity, gender, living situation, or case type.

Principal components analyses were performed on the relationships among the twelve family satisfaction questions at each interview wave. For each variable, the mean was substituted for missing data. Table 6.2 shows the single principal component with an eigenvalue greater than 1.0 in the baseline and Time 1 family satisfaction data, together with the loadings of the twelve questions on these principal components. As can be seen, the loadings of the scales on the

Table 6.2. Loading of Satisfaction-with-Family Questions on the Main Principal Components at Baseline and Time 1 (n = 248)

Variable	Baseline Interview*	Time 1 Interview*
How satisfied are you with:		
How close you feel to the rest of your family?	76	77
Your ability to say what you want in your family?	48	59
Your family's ability to try new things?	75	77
How fair the criticism is in your family?	50	53
The amount of time you spend with your family?	66	64
The way you talk together to solve family problems?	78	78
Your freedom to be alone when you want to?	48	48
How strictly you stay with assigned chores in your family?	60	64
Your family's acceptance of your friends?	52	66
How clear is it what your family expects of you?	69	70
How often you make decisions as a family, rather than individually?	70	82
The number of fun things your family does together?	67	74
Eigenvalue	4.94	5.63

*Decimal points omitted.

principal components were similar over time; each of the questions loaded highly and positively on each component. A regression factor score was created to summarize these data for the principal component at each time. Higher scores indicate more reported satisfaction with the family.

In preparing for our analyses of the impact of the FEI on the youths' reported satisfaction with their families, we compared ESI youths, youths not completing the FEI, and youths completing the FEI on fourteen entry variables (eight psychosocial, delinquency history, and abuse-neglect history varimax components and six demographic and referral history variables [age, gender, race, ethnicity, living situation, and diversion or other case]). The results indicated there were no significant differences among the three groups on any of these variables. Based on these results, it was not necessary to control statistically for possible differences at entry among these three groups before examining the Time 1 data on satisfaction with the family.

We completed an analysis of covariance comparing the three groups of youths on the summary score of satisfaction with the family, controlling for their satisfaction at their baseline interview. The analysis comparing FEI and ESI youths found a marginally significant difference ($F = 2.26$; df $=1,247$; $p < .10$ for a one-sided test of significance). The comparison between youths completing the FEI and those not completing the FEI was nonsignificant. Figure 6.1 provides a more graphic representation of the average scores for satisfaction with the family at Time 1 for ESI youths, youths completing the FEI, and youths not completing the FEI, which have been adjusted for their reported family satisfaction at baseline interview. As can be seen, ESI youths had the lowest scores, youths not completing the FEI the next lowest scores, and youths completing the FEI the highest reported satisfaction with their families.

Communication with Parents/Guardians

We also conducted a series of analyses involving project youths' responses to a series of questions probing their reported communication with adults in the household with a parenting role. The twenty-item Barnes and Olson (1982) parent-adolescent communication instrument was used (with permission) to collect these data (see

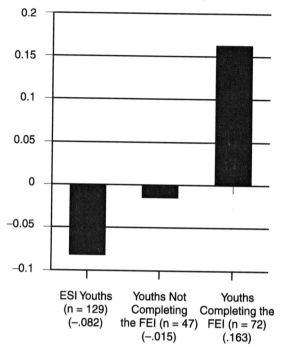

Figure 6.1. Adjusted Mean Values of Youth-Reported Family Satisfaction at First Follow-Up Interview for ESI Youths, Youths Not Completing the FEI, and Youths Completing the FEI

Appendix B). Again, since the youths' living circumstances changed significantly over time, the baseline and Time 1 communication information was studied. There were 218 instances in which baseline and Time 1 communication data were available for the same adult: 194 (89 percent) involved youths' reports of communication with mothers; 12 cases (5 percent), communication with grandmothers; 7 cases (3 percent), communication with aunts; 4 cases (2 percent), communication with fathers; and 1 case (< 1 percent), communication with an uncle. Because the vast majority of the communication data involved mothers, our analyses focused on that.

Field administration of the communication instrument indicated the youths had difficulties in responding to some questions. These were attributable to the reverse wording of a number of the questions and the language level and cultural relevance of some of the questions. Thus, we decided to compare the responses of ESI youths, youths not completing the FEI, and youths completing the FEI to each of the questions separately. Prior to these comparisons, a factor analysis was performed on these 194 youths' baseline psychosocial, delinquency history, and abuse-neglect history variables, similar to the one reported in Chapter 4. A discriminant analysis, comparing ESI youths, youths not completing the FEI, and youths completing the FEI, was performed on nine psychosocial, delinquency history, and abuse-neglect history varimax factors resulting from a factor analysis and on six demographic and referral history variables (age, gender, race, ethnicity, living situation, and diversion or other case). The results were as follows: Wilks' lambda = 0.902, chi-square = 19.10, df = 28, p = n.s. (function 1); Wilks' lambda = 0.980, chi-square = 3.70, df = 13, p = n.s. (function 2). In addition, there was only one significant difference among the three groups on any of the fifteen variables, which could have easily been produced by chance. Based on these results, we deemed it unnecessary to control statistically for possible differences at entry among these three groups before examining the Time 1 communication data.

Because male and female youths' reports of communication with their mothers could be expected to differ, we analyzed these data for the 194 cases overall and separately for male (n = 108) and female (n = 86) youths. Overall analyses indicated there were significant differences in reported communication across the ESI, FEI non-completers, and FEI completers on only two questions, no significant effects for the female youths, and only two significant effects for the male youths. These findings remained even after the youths' baseline responses to the communication questions were employed as covariates in the analyses. Since sixty analyses were completed, these differences could easily have been produced by chance and were not considered further.

INFLUENCE OF CHANGE IN PROJECT'S CLINICAL LEADERSHIP ON OUTCOMES

A further analysis was completed to determine if the change in the project's clinical leadership in March 1996 affected the youths' emotional/psychological functioning scores. The results indicated time of entry into the project did not have an appreciable effect on short-term or long-term emotional/psychological functioning.

SUMMARY OF FINDINGS

Overall, the results of our analyses indicate that the FEI did not influence the youths' emotional/psychological functioning over time, as reflected in the youths' responses to the SCL-90-R. However, there was some suggestion the FEI might have influenced the youths' reported satisfaction with their families between the baseline and first follow-up interview. The results here were marginally significant and in the theoretically expected direction across ESI youths, youths not completing the FEI, and youths completing the FEI. Should further replications of this intervention be undertaken, more robust, culturally and developmentally sensitive, and comprehensive assessments of the youths' functioning in this important area should be conducted.

Chapter 7

Conclusions and Directions
for the Future

In this chapter, we summarize and integrate the results reported in previous chapters. We also discuss the results of additional analyses on the cost-effectiveness of the Family Empowerment Intervention (FEI).

What did we learn from the over 850 in-depth interviews we completed for this project and the thousands of official records we reviewed? The results of the outcome analyses reported in Chapters 4 (crime/delinquency) and 5 (alcohol and other drug use) provide evidence in support of the efficacy of the FEI, particularly among youths who completed the intervention. As we discussed in Chapter 6, the results of our analyses of the FEI's impact on emotional/psychological functioning proved disappointing—with the exception of the youths' reported satisfaction with their families.

Hypothesis-consistent effects were found in regard to various recidivism and psychosocial outcome measures involving comparisons between Extended Services Intervention (ESI) and FEI youths and between youths not completing and completing the FEI. These results took into account group differences on a variety of demographic, psychosocial, offense history, and abuse-neglect history variables. The main hypothesis of the study was that empowering parents would improve client youths' behavior and psychosocial functioning—including reduced recidivism. The findings support this key hypothesis, and they indicate the promise of this intervention. (See Appendix C for a list of published articles resulting from the Youth Support Project [YSP].)

SHORT-TERM IMPACT OF THE FEI

The evidence for the deterrent effects of the FEI is particularly strong for the first twelve-month follow-up analyses (Time 1). The pattern of significant findings across diverse outcome measures of psychosocial functioning is impressive. As discussed in Chapters 4, 5, and 6, there were fourteen outcome variables in the study:

1. Emotional/psychological functioning, probed by the Symptom Check List-90-Revised (SCL-90-R; Derogatis, 1983)
2. New charges and new arrests
3. Five types of self-reported delinquency
4. Four types of alcohol or other drug use
5. Family satisfaction and communication

For outcome variables one through four, the effect of the intervention (FEI versus ESI) and the interaction of the intervention with case type were examined, yielding twenty-four tests of significance; for the family satisfaction and communication outcome variables, comparison between the FEI and ESI groups added two additional tests of significance.

The Bonferroni inequality (Miller, 1981) gives an upper bound of 1.00 as the probability that one or more of twenty-six tests of significance will be significant at the .05 level. Thus, it is not appropriate to claim that results are statistically significant by evaluating each test of significance as a separate study at the .05 level. One strategy for controlling for the probability of claiming significance by chance is to make a single, overall statement of significance for the entire study, with significance if any of the twenty-six tests achieve the .05/26 = .0019 level of significance. Such a strategy, however, penalizes a researcher for evaluating multiple outcomes and encourages fragmentation of reports. Miller (1981) proposed an intermediate strategy: grouping the tests into "families" and evaluating each family as a separate study at the .05 significance level, using the Bonferroni inequality. This provides a reasonable balance; it yields a small number of conclusions concerning substantively distinct objectives of research. Using this strategy, we grouped the twenty-six tests into six families:

1. FEI versus ESI on emotional/psychological functioning
2. FEI versus ESI on official records of offenses
3. FEI versus ESI on self-reported delinquency
4. FEI versus ESI on alcohol and other drug use
5. Family satisfaction and communication
6. The interaction of ESI versus FEI intervention with case type

Thus, these six families have one, two, five, four, two, and twelve tests of significance, respectively. For testing each family separately, Holm's (1979) improvement to the Bonferroni inequality was used. If the most significant test is significant by the Bonferroni criterion .05/(number of tests), the next most significant test is tested at the level of significance .05/(number of tests – 1), and so on. When the results were evaluated using these levels of significance, which were more stringent than .05, some results were still significant. Compared to the ESI, the FEI did not have an appreciable effect on emotional/ psychological functioning or on self-reported delinquency. However, it was associated with reductions in drug use during Time 1, specifically in self-reported frequency of getting very high or drunk on alcohol and self-reported frequency of marijuana use. The interaction analyses did not reveal any substantial differences between the effect of FEI relative to ESI for diversion as distinguished from nondiversion youths.

Although the comparison between FEI completers and non-completers was post hoc, it is appropriate to evaluate them taking account of multiple tests of significance. Following the pattern of "families" specified in the twelve-month follow-up analyses, there are five families of outcome measures:

1. Emotional/psychological functioning
2. Official records of new charges and new arrests
3. Self-reported delinquency
4. Alcohol/other drug use
5. Family satisfaction and communication

Except for family satisfaction and communication, each of these families included both short- and long-term outcomes, so the number of tests in the respective families are two, four, ten, eight, and two. When the results were reviewed, some achieved statistical significance even using these more challenging significance levels. For official records of new charges and new arrests, the twelve-month outcome data showed FEI completers had lower rates than non-completers. In addition, for self-reported delinquency, the twelve-month outcome findings indicated FEI completers reported lower rates of participation in crimes against persons and total delinquency than noncompleters.

The comparisons of youths who did and did not complete the intervention, and other comparisons discussed in Chapters 4 and 5, show clearly that the FEI's success was due to those youths who completed the intervention. Youths who did not complete the intervention did not differ from ESI youths. This supports the efficacy of the intervention. An alternative explanation is that youths did better because they were amenable to intervention rather than as the effect of the intervention. However, if that were the case, one would expect that there would be other differences in baseline characteristics, which we did not find.

LONG-TERM IMPACT OF THE FEI

As discussed in Chapters 4 and 5, the results of our long-term self-reported delinquency analyses indicated that youths completing the FEI had significantly lower reported rates of crimes against persons, drug sales, and total delinquency than youths not completing the FEI. Again, these results took into account group differences on a variety of demographic, psychosocial, offense history, and abuse-neglect history variables. In addition, the findings held up under further study of possible interaction effects. They provide evidence in support of the efficacy and sustained effect of the FEI. Further, as discussed in more detail in Chapter 4, the differences in number of new charges and number of new arrests were in the predicted direction. The FEI youths who completed the intervention had marginally significantly fewer transformed new charges and very close to significantly fewer transformed new arrests than youths not completing the FEI. Importantly, there were no significant interactions of group differences with length of follow-up, which indicates that overall differences among groups did not vary substantially for different lengths of follow-up.

These results support the efficacy of the intervention (although at a more modest level than in the twelve-month official record outcome analyses) and its sustained effect. Again, an alternative explanation is that youths did better because they were amenable to intervention rather than as the effect of the intervention. However, we did not find other differences in baseline characteristics to support that explanation.

Since the intervention was designed to be short term, and no additional services were systematically provided following completion of the FEI, the long-term outcome effects we found were particularly gratifying. The long-term recidivism and psychosocial functioning outcome findings are particularly important in light of experience that the salutary effects of intervention programs for high-risk youths are often short-lived (University of Colorado, 1999). The treatment or intervention gains of most programs are lost after participation in the intervention or soon thereafter.

COULD PROJECT REFERRALS TO SERVICES ACCOUNT FOR ITS IMPACT, NOT THE FEI?

As discussed in Chapter 1, following baseline data collection, youths and their families, regardless of whether they were assigned to receive FEI or ESI services, were able to use an extensive resource file developed by project staff in order to gain referrals to other agencies in the community. This resource system enabled project staff, including field consultants, to provide families with information about different community agencies, and staff members assisted families in obtaining appropriate referrals to meet their needs. Nevertheless, both the field consultants' referrals and their assistance in making contact with agencies raise the possibility that the delinquency/crime and psychosocial outcomes identified in our analyses could be attributed to differences in extent of referrals to other services. We examined this issue by comparing the responses of ESI youths, youths not completing the FEI, and youths completing the FEI to a series of questions probing their receiving various services during their first, second, and third follow-up periods. The results of these analyses clearly indicated that referral differences could not be considered responsible for any of the delinquency/crime and psychosocial outcomes identified in the analyses reported in Chapters 4, 5, and 6. Table 7.1 presents these comparisons for the service experiences reported by the youths during their first follow-up interview. As can be seen, the only differences among the three groups related to their

TABLE 7.1. Percentage of ESI Youths, FEI Noncompleters, and FEI Completers Who Reported Receiving Various Services During the First Follow-Up Period

Since Baseline Interview, Youth Reported	ESI Youths (n = 142)	FEI Non-Completers (n = 55)	FEI Completers (n = 73)	Chi-Square Value
Was arrested	53.5%	65.5%	35.6%	11.18***
Spent time in a juvenile detention center	38.0%	34.5%	17.8%	4.69
Spent time in jail	9.9%	10.9%	11.0%	0.00
Spent time in prison	0.7%	–	1.4%	0.76
Spent time in a residential commitment program	10.6%	14.5%	6.8%	2.04
Was put on nonsecure home detention (including electronic monitoring)	13.5% (n = 141)	20.0%	16.4%	0.27
Was put on probation or community control	35.9%	34.5%	30.1%	0.28
Spent time in a hospital for a physical problem	6.3%	10.9%	6.8%	0.66
Spent time in a hospital for a mental/psychological/emotional problem	8.5%	3.6%	4.1%	0.02
Spent time in a hospital for an alcohol or drug problem	2.1% (n = 141)	3.6%	–	2.70
Spent time in a residential alcohol/other drug program	2.1%	3.6%	1.4%	0.70
Spent time in any other closed facility or program	5.6%	–	2.7%	1.53
Was in an outpatient drug treatment or counseling program	3.5%	1.8%	1.4%	0.04
Saw an outpatient counselor, such as a psychologist or psychiatrist	16.2%	9.1%	4.1%	1.33
Spent time in any other outpatient program	1.4%	3.7%	1.4%	0.73

*.10 > p > .05
**p < .05
***p < .01
****p < .001

involvement with the justice system, which was not part of the project's referral protocol. Similar results were obtained in the analyses of the youths' reported service experiences during their second and third follow-up periods (see Appendixes D and E, respectively, for these tables).

COST-SAVING BENEFITS OF THE FEI

The benefits of the FEI in regard to reduced involvement with the justice system and improvements in psychosocial functioning in the areas of reported delinquent/criminal behavior and alcohol and other drug use (measured by self-report and hair test data), are critical aspects of its contribution to individual, family, community, and public health. An additional area of benefits concerns the cost savings to the justice system from implementing the intervention. Such information is very important to policymakers and agency directors trying to improve the behavior of troubled youths in the most cost-efficient manner.

We examined this issue by estimating the direct cost savings to the juvenile justice system by providing FEI services to diversion-eligible youths in Hillsborough County, Florida, where the intervention was implemented and evaluated. This analysis incorporated information on the costs of new arrests and incarceration of youths receiving ESI and FEI services during each twelve-month period following random assignment. The results of this analysis were most revealing. They document that the justice system can anticipate substantial direct cost savings from use of this intervention.

In our cost-benefit analysis, we estimated the three-year cumulative direct cost savings to the Hillsborough County juvenile justice system by providing FEI services to the 3,600 diversion-eligible youths who are processed each year at the Juvenile Assessment Center (JAC). Diversion (nonserious offender) cases were chosen because they represented the least costly group of offenders to process and involve in service programs. Justice system processing costs were provided by the following agencies: the Hillsborough County

Sheriff's Office, the State's Attorney's Office, the Public Defender's Office, the 13th Judicial Circuit Court Administrator's Office, and the Florida Department of Juvenile Justice. (We are deeply grateful to Ms. Pat Marsicano, Hillsborough County Anti-Drug Alliance, for providing these data.) In addition, we developed cost figures for implementing the FEI: $1,154 per family (based on $24,000 yearly salary and 18 percent fringe benefits for each field consultant, cost of pager and mobile telephone, supervision and training costs, and travel expenses to the site of family meetings). For this analysis, we used nontransformed new arrest rates for FEI youths compared to ESI youths in each cumulative period.

In regard to incarceration costs, from justice system records we determined the number of days ESI and FEI youths were incarcerated during each cumulative twelve-month period following random assignment to the ESI or FEI group. Some youths were incarcerated in county jail, juvenile justice residential commitment programs, or Florida Department of Corrections prisons, each of which has different daily costs. However, all incarcerated youths spent time in juvenile detention facilities and for many youths juvenile detention represented their only periods of incarceration. Hence, for illustrative purposes, we used the daily cost for placement in a juvenile detention center ($95; personal communication from Florida Department of Juvenile Justice, August 4, 2000) to calculate the average incarceration cost per category of youths.

The results of our analysis indicate that, taking into account the cost of providing FEI services, implementing the FEI for 3,600 diversion cases processed at the JAC would save the Hillsborough County juvenile justice system $4.7 million in cumulative direct costs over a three-year period. Not surprisingly, since the FEI is an overlay service, the year-1 costs involved in providing FEI services exceed those of providing current ninety-day diversion services. By year 2, due primarily to lower incarceration rates for youths provided FEI services, youths receiving FEI services are projected to save the juvenile justice system $934,139. By the end of year 3, the cumulative cost savings to the justice system as a result of providing FEI services rises to $4.7 million. Table 7.2 presents these results.

TABLE 7.2. Three-Year Cumulative Juvenile Justice System Direct Cost Savings Associated with Providing FEI Services to Diversion Cases

Costs	Youths Placed in a 90-Day Diversion Program	Youths Provided FEI Services
One-year		
Initial[a]	$ 6,980,400	$11,134,800
New arrest[b]	6,055,165	5,364,663
Incarceration	6,703,200	5,506,200
Total	$19,738,765	$22,005,663
Two-year cumulative		
Initial[a]	$ 6,980,400	$11,134,800
New arrest[b]	11,101,136	11,313,597
Incarceration	23,221,800	17,920,800
Total	$41,303,336	$40,369,197
Three-year cumulative		
Initial[a]	$ 6,980,400	$11,134,800
New arrest[b]	16,147,106	13,863,140
Incarceration	47,982,600	41,416,200
Total	$71,110,106	$66,414,140

[a] Includes arrest costs, state's attorney's costs, public defender costs, judicial costs, and Department of Juvenile Justice costs (excluding detention costs). The initial costs for youths receiving FEI services also include the expense of providing the intervention ($1,154 per family).
[b] Includes arrest costs, state's attorney's costs, public defender costs, judicial costs, and Department of Juvenile Justice costs (including detention costs).

The data are even more impressive when one considers, as noted above, that many other, nonestimated indirect cost benefits could also be expected to occur as a result of providing FEI services, such as

1. improvements in the quality of family life,
2. improvements in the behavior of other family members toward one another and in the community,
3. reduced family use of various public resources (e.g., welfare, health),

4. reduced productivity losses due to alcohol/other drug abuse or
   mental health disorders,
5. reduced productivity losses due to incarceration or involvement
   in careers in crime,
6. reduced victimization of others.

HOW COULD THE FEI BE IMPROVED?

Although our outcome data provide a convincing case for the
promise of the FEI, the results, as well as our own experience, indicate a number of ways in which the intervention can be improved.

Required Participation

There is a growing literature documenting that gains in substance
abuse and other treatment are more dependent on the length of treatment and the quality of treatment services than on whether the client
voluntarily entered the treatment program. Much of this literature de-
rives from studies of substance abuse treatment outcomes for adults
(Leukefeld, 1991; Wexler et al., 1999). Some concern has been expressed regarding the use of coercion in the treatment of drug-
involved adolescents. In a recent study of adolescent alcohol/other
drug abuse treatment conducted for the Center for Substance Abuse
Treatment, Winters (1999:xvii) argued against explicitly or implic-
itly coercing adolescents into treatment, asserting that "coercive
pressure to seek treatment is not generally sensitive to the behavior
change process." Instead, treatment providers were urged to identify
motivational barriers to change and use various strategies to engage
youths reluctant to pursue behavioral change. At the same time, the
use of creatively applied legal pressure to participate in treatment
should not be discounted.

Throughout the clinical trial of the FEI, family participation was
voluntary. Although we achieved a 53 percent graduation rate, our
sense (although not scientifically tested) is that court-ordered participation in intervention services could have increased family engagement in the intervention and the period of time families received
those services.

Booster Sessions

Although our clinical trial of the FEI did not do so, we strongly recommend that, wherever possible, booster sessions be made available to families receiving FEI services. Such sessions could be made available to families that have completed the intervention, as well as those families that have stopped participating in the intervention for such reasons as work schedules. These sessions, periodically provided for a brief time, could be helpful in assisting graduated families to maintain the gains they made when receiving FEI services and to address any new issues they may be facing. For families that have not completed the FEI, booster sessions could address current issues they are facing, as well as provide an opportunity to reengage in intervention services. The long-term impact of the FEI was gratifying given that no booster sessions were provided to families assigned to receive intervention services. We think it is highly likely that even more impact would have been found if such sessions had been available.

During the clinical trial of the FEI, upon completion of FEI services, or following closing of a family's case, efforts were made to maintain contact by telephone every four to six weeks. These calls with parents/family members were used to maintain contact with the families, verify their current address, and monitor what was happening to each family after the intensive intervention period ended. The contacts calls were also used to identify those families that were in need of further assistance by a field consultant, either by telephone or at home. For families that were again experiencing significant difficulty dealing with their child or were undergoing a period of extreme stress, the case was discussed at the project's weekly meeting with clinical staff. The project's clinical policy was first to see if it was possible to make a referral to another agency ("system fit"). Although field consultants were trained to provide intervention services, there were a number of occasions when they needed to draw on community resources for additional treatment services for families. Examples of such occasions were assisting a parent to enter a substance abuse treatment program or a psychiatric facility and assisting a youth in accessing academic tutoring or positive recreational outlets. As noted in Chapter 2, the project developed and maintained an extensive, current description of available community services for making such referrals. When deemed appropriate by clinical staff, a field consultant would contact the family to obtain more information on the nature of the service need; following review of the case with clinical staff, it was possible to arrange for the family to receive additional FEI services. While, in practice, relatively few families received these additional FEI services (fewer than fifteen), we believe providing routine booster sessions to FEI families would reduce their problems and improve their rate of resuming the intervention.

Efforts were also made to contact ESI families by telephone every four to six weeks. These calls with parents/family members were used to maintain contact with the families and verify their current address. Family requests for service referrals were followed up by project staff.

Continuing Efforts at Enrollment and Involvement

Our experience indicated that enrolling and involving families in the FEI were continuing needs. Self-termination presented an ongoing challenge to the field consultants and clinical staff. In Chapter 2, we discussed the strategies of engagement and joining that field consultants used to retain families in the intervention. The following examples of intervention successes and challenges illustrate the need to regard enrollment and engagement as ongoing issues.

Families Completing the FEI

Field consultant Gina. My first family to graduate showed commitment to the project from the very beginning. When I made my first call to them, they were eager to hear more about the project and asked a lot of questions. Our first meeting was scheduled within a week of our telephone call, and they kept their initial appointment, at which all family members were present. During our first meeting, family members committed themselves to the project for the next ten to fifteen weeks and to two or three meetings a week. Each person was eager to get started. The family members came up with attainable goals for the entire family as well as for themselves. Once the goals were set, the family began to take action. Few meetings were canceled. When they were canceled, it was due to such reasons as work or illness. Each family member was present for all meetings. As the weeks went on, when there was not a scheduled meeting, the family continued to have meetings on their own.

At about the eighth week, I had the family check their progress to see where they wanted to go from there. They all agreed that changes were being made. The parents were feeling more empowered and were setting boundaries for the client youth. Mom and Dad were sharing the rule making and the responsibilities for discipline. The family had also commented that they were having fun. This progress could be seen on the videotapes. The client youth's progress was terrific. When I first started working with this family, the client youth was making poor grades and had no real goals for the future. By the end of the intervention, the client youth had pulled all his Ds and Fs up to As, Bs, or Cs. He was even sharing his ideas with his parents about going to trade school. The client youth was taking responsibility for his own actions and choices and was obeying the rules his parents had set. This family showed significant changes throughout the intervention. Each family member stayed committed to the project and worked hard to make positive changes within the family.

Field consultant Tim. This family involved a single parent and her daughter. The daughter entered the project as a result of being arrested on a shoplifting charge. As I began working with this family, I learned that there were several issues facing them. These issues included the client youth's using drugs (her boyfriend of two years was a drug dealer) and being on the verge of expulsion from school. In addition, her mother was chronically depressed and had been out of work for six weeks.

Initially, the family was not excited about having another "social service worker" come into their home. In fact, there were many early cancellations of meetings by the mother. Fortunately, once we really got into the intervention the progress was extraordinary. In particular, changes started to occur as the family watched their own interactions on videotape and critiqued their interaction and communication patterns. During the course of our meetings, the client youth was expelled from regular school and was placed in an alternative school—but her potential would soon come through. Mother's and daughter's boundaries became better defined, and changes could be seen on a daily basis. Mom went back to work and developed a social life. She cautiously started dating again and doing things for herself. She began to stay firm with her rules, and follow with both positive and negative reinforcement. This is best illustrated by her buying her daughter a puppy when she returned to her regular high school six months after their completion of the program. Likewise, the daughter began to seek new friends that were more appropriate for her. She excelled in school after her mother took more control of the situation, is currently back in regular school, and is due to graduate on time next year. She stopped sharing clothes with her mother and began to take on more responsibilities around the home. After an initially poor reaction to her mother's dating, the client youth became supportive of her mother's seeing other men. She currently is not only doing well in school but holds a job in a fried chicken restaurant, where she has been working for the past seven months. From time to time, I bump into her while she is working. This family made incredible changes, many of which were a direct result of our meetings. Additionally, they continued making positive changes after graduation, which shows how much they had internalized new problem-solving processes. This is a family I have seen in the community (e.g., at the grocery store), and they continue to credit the Youth Support Project for their changes.

Families Failing to Complete the FEI

Field consultant Vincent. The client youth was living with his biological mother and two sisters, one older and one younger. I made several visits to the housing project where the client youth and family resided only to find no one at home. I eventually made contact with the mother and client youth after the third visit. Mother stated that she could not stop styling hair (a primary source of income at the time) to commit to family meetings in the afternoons or evenings. She indicated that I was welcome to visit the client youth any time because "someone needs to talk to him." Mother made it clear that her first and foremost priority was to continue to style hair in order to have an income to provide food, shelter, and other basic essentials of life to maintain the family's standard of living. I concluded that the mother wanted an outside source to solve her family's problems, particularly regarding the client youth's inappropriate behavior (e.g., smoking marijuana, selling drugs, unwilling to work, unwilling to attend school on a regular basis, and refusing to initiate a proper transition to adulthood). During several visits and conversations with the client youth, he stated that he and his mother had not been communicating in the past few months. In addition, I learned that the mother wanted the youth out of the home because he would be 18 soon, and she had grown very frustrated and tired of his behavior. Also, mother did not condone his behavior, but she did acknowledge that he was only acting as he saw others in the neighborhood do.

After several attempts to coordinate meetings with the client youth and mother had failed, the client youth was arrested on pending charges. I made several scheduled visits to the county jail to meet the client youth. Mother made very few visits to the jail, and I found it very difficult to bring the client youth and mother together for meetings. Following the client youth's release from jail, he and the rest of the family moved, leaving no forwarding address. I finally had to close this case.

Field consultant Jennifer. This family consisted of a fifteen-year-old male and his sixty-five-year-old grandfather. The client youth's mother had died when he was seven, and he had been raised by his grandmother until her death one year ago. His father was a drug addict who had been in and out of the client youth's life, as well as in and out of prison. The family lived in a lower class neighborhood and their only income was from disability and social security checks. The client youth's offense was burglary, and he was attending alternative school because of excessive fighting in a traditional school. He was very bright but did not apply himself in school. He often talked about gang activity and bragged about the crimes he had committed but had not been caught for. He also spoke of his older brothers, whom he referred to as the "biggest drug dealers in town."

The grandfather was raised on a farm with fifteen brothers and sisters and was unable to read or write. He worked in construction his whole life until an accident left his hand crippled. He had been raising the client youth on his own since the death of his wife, and had had very little to do with the youth's previous upbringing. His main issues with the youth were completing his chores and obtaining a good education. This family appeared to be interested in the intervention at the start, but the fact that there were only two of them and the grandfather could not read, write, or even draw or build things due to his crippled hand made performing intervention activities quite difficult. Accordingly, there was more verbal interaction than usual. It became obvious that the grandfather had very little experience raising children, that he expected little more than respect from the client youth, and that he did not really impose any rules on him. Since the death of his wife, the grandfather was gone most of the time, leaving the youth on his own. It was also very obvious that both were still suffering from the death of the grandmother, especially the client youth, who had lost his "second" mother.

After a couple of months, the grandfather stopped coming to meetings entirely (his attendance had been sporadic before that). The client youth was willing to continue with the intervention, but could not get his grandfather to commit. The grandfather had a girlfriend whom he preferred to spend time with, and this caused a lot of resentment in the client youth toward his grandfather. There was never much of a connection between the two, and even less of one after the death of the grandmother. Although the grandfather was concerned about the client youth and his future, he had no parenting skills and was not willing to take the time to learn how to improve their relationship.

NEXT STEPS

The recidivism and psychosocial functioning outcome analyses completed for this project indicate the efficacy of the FEI, its sustained effect, and its cost-effectiveness. We hope other jurisdictions will be interested in implementing this promising in-home service. As noted in Chapters 1 and 2, one advantage of the FEI is that it does not rely on trained professionals delivering services, which decreases its cost considerably. For example, compared to the average cost of approximately $6,000 for families receiving multisystemic therapy (see Chapter 1), the FEI costs less than $1,200 per family. The FEI provides a cost-effective alternative to professionally driven services and could be of great benefit to juvenile justice practitioners in their desire to serve as many families as possible within limited budgets.

Another advantage of the FEI is that it is well documented. The FEI manual, one product of this National Institute on Drug Abuse funded project, consists of two separate parts: an implementation manual and an activities manual. (Please contact senior author regarding this manual.) The FEI manual is action oriented. It was written to provide its users with "hands on" information and material that will enable them to implement this service. The manual is written for the paraprofessional personnel who will be implementing the FEI and their clinical supervisors and trainers. Its purposes are to provide (1) an understanding of the theoretical foundations, policies, and procedures relating to the intervention, and (2) information on the strategies, activities, and practices involved in implementing this intervention. While the manual is designed to stand alone, carrying out the intervention successfully requires the selection of effective and committed personnel, their adequate training and clinical supervision, and ongoing efforts to ensure the integrity of the intervention. Our clinical trial of the FEI found that adherence to these ingredients was essential to the successful implementation of this intervention.

The implementation manual provides the theoretical foundations for the FEI, together with the policies and practices involved in carrying it out. The activities manual presents specific games, artistic projects, and exercises in which family members can engage to facilitate achieving the goals of the intervention. The activities manual evolved from our early experience in implementing the FEI, which indicated that many of the families we worked with did not respond well to verbal interaction and sharing of feelings and information. We found that the various activities often provide an essential way to bring to light problems the families are experiencing in a manner they can directly understand. The FEI implementation and activities manuals were designed to be complementary documents. We have found that project field consultants carry the activities manual with them in the field to plan specific activities for family meetings or to use it in setting up or providing instructions to families involved in specific games, exercises, and the like.

The FEI is a low-cost, innovative service for arrested youths and their families. It is particularly useful for minority and inner-city youths and their families, who have historically been underserved (Arcia, 1993; Dembo and Seeberger, 1999). Many of these families often lack the resources to access community-based services. When seeking publicly funded services, they are often required to visit program offices at some distance from their homes. Culturally sensitive staff, providing in-home services, can help eliminate barriers to treatment and meet families on their own terms.

Juvenile justice systems throughout the United States are experiencing increased workload and resource pressures. Juvenile crime and its effects continue to increase, and there is growing awareness of the magnitude of these and related problems among various high-risk groups (Butts and Harrell, 1998). The FEI is an informed, effective response to these issues. By seeking to strengthen families, the intervention helps sustain the most basic of our social institutions.

Appendix A

Time 1 Summary Measures for Six Sets of Major Variables

Delinquency Referral History

A principal components analysis was completed on seven delinquency referral variables to see how they clustered:

1. Property felony offenses (e.g., burglary)
2. Felony violence offenses (e.g., robbery)
3. Felony drug offenses
4. Violent misdemeanor offenses (e.g., assault)
5. Misdemeanor property offenses (e.g., retail theft)
6. Misdemeanor public disorder offenses (e.g., trespassing)
7. Misdemeanor drug offenses

The initial solution, involving two factors with eigenvalues greater than 1.0, was rotated to varimax criteria for factor clarity. The two factors that were identified in these data were (1) violence, property, and public disorder offenses, and (2) drug offenses. Based on these results, regression factor scores were calculated (Kim and Mueller, 1978). Higher scores on each factor indicated more frequent referrals.

Family Problems

A principal components analysis was also completed on variables measuring family members'

1. Alcohol abuse
2. Other drug abuse
3. Emotional/mental health problems
4. Contact with the justice system (been arrested, held in jail/detention, adjudicated delinquent or convicted of a crime, put on community control or probation, or sent to a training school or prison)

In this analysis, two principal components were identified with eigenvalues above 1.0. These components were rotated using varimax criteria for factor clarity. The two factors that were identified in the data were (1) family member involvement with the justice system and (2) family member alcohol abuse, other drug abuse, or mental health problems. Summary regression factor scores were created for further analysis. For each factor, higher scores indicated more family problems.

Friends' Problem Behavior

A principal components analysis was completed on the friends' substance use and justice system contact variables as a data-reduction technique (Kim and Mueller, 1978) and to see how they clustered. (Low-frequency behaviors, such as reported friends' use of heroin, were excluded from this factor analysis.) Two principal components had eigenvalues above 1.0, and they were rotated using varimax criteria for factor clarity. The two factors that were identified in the data were (1) friends' involvement with the justice system and (2) friends' drug use (alcohol, marijuana/hashish, hallucinogens, cocaine). Regression factor scores (Kim and Mueller, 1978) were created as a summary measure for further analysis. The higher the score, the more the reported friends' involvement with the justice system and/or drug use. (In our twelve-month and long-term psychosocial outcome studies, the criminal justice variable reflecting "being sent to a training school or prison" was more strongly related to the friends' drug use factor.)

Self-Reported Physical Abuse

As a data-reduction procedure, a principal components analysis was undertaken on the six physical abuse items:

1. Been beaten or *really* hurt by being hit (but not with anything)
2. Been beaten or hit with a whip, strap, or belt
3. Been beaten or hit with something "hard" (like a club or stick)
4. Been shot with a gun, injured with a knife, or had some other "weapon" used against them
5. Been hurt badly enough to require (need) a doctor or bandages or other medical treatment
6. Spent time in a hospital because they were physically injured

Two principal components with eigenvalues greater than 1.0 were identified in these data. These two components were varimax rotated for factor clarity. The two factors that were identified were (1) serious physical harm (above listed items 3 to 6 loaded highly on this factor), and (2) been beaten or hit (items 1 and 2 loaded highly on this factor). On the basis of these results, regression factor scores were created. For each factor, higher scores indicated more modes of physical harm claimed.

Self-Reported Delinquent Behavior

As discussed in Chapter 3, the National Youth Survey Delinquency Scale items (Elliott et al., 1983) were used in developing summary measures on the following behaviors:

1. General theft crimes
2. Crimes against persons
3. Index offenses
4. Drug sales
5. Total delinquency

Since the range of responses to the items comprising the five self-reported delinquency scales was large, ranging from no activity to hundreds (and in a few cases thousands), analysis of the frequency data as an interval scale was not appropriate as a measure of involvement in delinquency/crime. Raw numbers of offenses do form an interval scale, which might be useful if one were predicting crime rates for populations. However, the difference between no offense and 1 offense is not the same as the difference between 99 and 100 offenses in terms of involvement. A transformation was employed so that equal intervals on the transformed scale would represent equal differences in involvement. We interpreted the differences between 1 and 10, 10 and 100, and 100 and 1,000 offenses as being comparable. Accordingly, we log transformed the number of offenses for each scale to the base 10.

For any base, logarithms exist for all positive numbers. The choice of base does not matter if the logarithms are analyzed by a statistical procedure invariant under linear transformation, such as analysis of variance, multiple regression, discriminant analysis, or factor analysis. However, regardless of the base, the logarithm of 0 does not exist. Some other method must be employed to determine the score assigned to no offenses. For any base, 0 is the logarithm of the value 1, and 1 is the logarithm of the base. If the difference from "base" offenses (10 in this study) to 1 offense is assigned the difference in logarithm scores of 1 and 0, this provides a unit of measurement for assigning a score even lower than 0—a negative number—to no offenses. In this study a score of -1 was assigned. This evaluates the difference between no offense and 1 offense as equal in importance as the difference between 1 offense and 10, or between 10 offenses and 100.

Emotional/Psychological Functioning

As discussed in Chapter 3, the Symptom Check List (SCL-90-R; Derogatis, 1983) probes problems in nine domains:

1. Somatization
2. Obsessive-compulsive
3. Interpersonal sensitivity
4. Depression
5. Anxiety
6. Hostility
7. Phobic anxiety
8. Paranoid ideation
9. Psychoticism

A principal components analysis was performed on the SCL-90-R T scores for the nine scales to see how they clustered. One principal component had an eigenvalue greater than 1.0. Each of the scales loaded significantly on this principal component. Based on this result, regression factor scores were created summarizing these data. The higher the score, the more emotional/psychological problems.

Appendix B

Parent-Adolescent Communication
(Adolescent and Mother Form)

Response Choices				
1	**2**	**3**	**4**	**5**
Strongly Disagree	**Moderately Disagree**	**Neither Agree Nor Disagree**	**Moderately Agree**	**Strongly Agree**

___ 1. I can discuss my beliefs with my mother without feeling restrained or embarrassed.

___ 2. Sometimes I have trouble believing everything my mother tells me. (Reverse scored)

___ 3. My mother is always a good listener.

___ 4. I am sometimes afraid to ask my mother for what I want. (Reverse scored)

___ 5. My mother has a tendency to say things to me which would be better left unsaid. (Reverse scored)

___ 6. My mother can tell how I am feeling without asking.

___ 7. I am very satisfied with how my mother and I talk together.

___ 8. If I were in trouble, I could tell my mother.

___ 9. I openly show affection to my mother.

___10. When we are having a problem, I often give my mother the silent treatment. (Reverse scored)

___11. I am careful about what I say to my mother. (Reverse scored)

___12. When talking to my mother, I have a tendency to say things that would be better left unsaid. (Reverse scored)

___13. When I ask questions, I get honest answers from my mother.

___14. My mother tries to understand my point of view.

___15. There are topics I avoid discussing with my mother. (Reverse scored)

___16. I find it easy to discuss problems with my mother.

___17. It is very easy for me to express all my true feelings to my mother.

___18. My mother nags/bothers me. (Reverse scored)

___19. My mother insults me when she is angry with me. (Reverse scored)

___20. I don't think I can tell my mother how I really feel about some things. (Reverse scored)

Source: Barnes and Olson, 1982. Copyright 1982 Life Innovations, Inc., P.O. Box 190, Minneapolis, MN 55440. For more information, visit <www.lifeinnovations.com>.

Appendix C

Publications Resulting from the Youth Support Project and Family Empowerment Intervention

Cervenka, K. A., R. Dembo, and C. H. Brown (1996). A family empowerment intervention for families of juvenile offenders. *Aggression and Violent Behavior: A Review Journal* 1: 205-216.

Dembo, R., K. A. Cervenka, B. Hunter, W. Wang, and J. Schmeidler (1999). Engaging high risk families in community-based intervention services. *Aggression and Violence: A Review Journal* 4: 41-58.

Dembo, R., G. DuDell, S. Livingston, and J. Schmeidler (2001). Family Empowerment Intervention: Conceptual foundation and clinical practices. *Journal of Offender Rehabilitation* 33: 1-31.

Dembo, R., K. Pacheco, J. Schmeidler, L. Fisher, and S. Cooper (1997). Drug use and delinquent behavior among high risk youths. *Journal of Child and Adolescent Substance Abuse* 6: 1-25.

Dembo, R., K. Pacheco, J. Schmeidler, G. Ramirez-Garnica, J. Guida, and A. Rahman (1998). A further study of gender differences in service needs among youths entering a juvenile assessment center. *Journal of Child and Adolescent Substance Abuse* 7: 49-77.

Dembo, R., G. Ramirez-Garnica, M. Rollie, and J. Schmeidler (2000). Impact of a family empowerment intervention on youth recidivism. *Journal of Offender Rehabilitation* 30: 59-98.

Dembo, R., G. Ramirez-Garnica, M. Rollie, J. Schmeidler, S. Livingston, and A. Hartsfield (2000). Youth recidivism 12 months after a family empowerment intervention: Final report. *Journal of Offender Rehabilitation* 31: 29-65.

Dembo, R., G. Ramirez-Garnica, J. Schmeidler, M. Rollie, S. Livingston, and A. Hartsfield (2001). Long-term impact of a Family Empowerment Intervention on juvenile offender recidivism. *Journal of Offender Rehabilitation* 33: 33-57.

Dembo, R., J. Schmeidler, K. Pacheco, S. Cooper, and L. W. Williams (1997). The relationships between youths' identified substance use, mental health or other problems at a juvenile assessment center and their referrals to needed services. *Journal of Child and Adolescent Substance Abuse* 6: 23-54.

Dembo, R., J. Schmeidler, W. Seeberger, M. Shemwell, L. Klein, M. Rollie, K. Pacheco, S. Livingston, and W. Wothke (2001). Long-term impact of a Family Empowerment Intervention on juvenile offender psychosocial functioning. *Journal of Offender Rehabilitation* 33: 59-109.

Dembo, R., W. Seeberger, M. Shemwell, J. Schmeidler, L. Klein, M. Rollie, K. Pacheco, A. Hartsfield, and W. Wothke (2000). Psychosocial functioning among juvenile offenders 12 months after family empowerment intervention. *Journal of Offender Rehabilitation* 32: 1-56.

Dembo, R., M. Shemwell, J. Guida, J. Schmeidler, W. Baumgartner, G. Ramirez-Garnica, and W. Seeberger (1999). Comparison of self-report, urine sample, and hair testing for drug use: A longitudinal study. In T. Mieczkowski (Ed.), *Drug testing methods: Assessment and evaluation* (pp. 91-107). New York: CRC Press.

Dembo, R., M. Shemwell, J. Guida, J. Schmeidler, K. Pacheco, and W. Seeberger (1998). A longitudinal study of the impact of a family empowerment intervention on juvenile offender psychosocial functioning: A first assessment. *Journal of Child and Adolescent Substance Abuse* 8: 15-54.

Dembo, R., M. Shemwell, K. Pacheco, W. Seeberger, M. Rollie, J. Schmeidler, and W. Wothke (2000), A longitudinal study of the impact of a Family Empowerment Intervention on juvenile offender psychosocial functioning: An expanded assessment. *Journal of Child and Adolescent Substance Abuse* 10: 1-7.

Dembo, R., W. Wothke, W. Seeberger, M. Shemwell, K. Pacheco, M. Rollie, J. Schmeidler, L. Klein, A. Hartsfield, and S. Livingston (2000). Testing a model of the influence of family problem factors on high risk youths' troubled behavior: A three-wave longitudinal study. *Journal of Psychoactive Drugs* 32: 55-65.

Dembo, R., W. Wothke, W. Seeberger, M. Shemwell, K. Pacheco, M. Rollie, J. Schmeidler, L. Klein, S. Livingston, and A. Hartsfield (in press). Testing a longitudinal model of the relationships among high risk youths' drug sales, drug use, and participation in index crimes, *Journal of Child and Adolescent Substance Abuse*.

Dembo, R., W. Wothke, M. Shemwell, K. Pacheco, W. Seeberger, M. Rollie, and J. Schmeidler (2000). A structural model of the influence of family problems and child abuse factors on serious delinquency among youths processed at a juvenile assessment center. *Journal of Child and Adolescent Substance Abuse* 10: 17-31.

Dembo, R., W. Wothke, M. Shemwell, K. Pacheco, W. Seeberger, M. Rollie, J. Schmeidler, L. Klein, A. Hartsfield, and S. Livingston (2000). Testing a longitudinal model of the influence of family problem factors on high risk youths' troubled behavior: A replication and update. *Journal of Child and Adolescent Substance Abuse* 10: 9-22.

Appendix D

Percentage of ESI Youths, FEI Noncompleters, and FEI Completers Who Reported Receiving Various Services During the Second Follow-Up Period

Since Baseline Interview, Youth Reported	ESI Youths (n = 89)	FEI Non-Completers (n = 30)	FEI Completers (n = 51)	Chi-Square Value
Was arrested	33.7%	43.3%	37.3%	0.20
Spent time in a juvenile detention center	19.1%	20.0%	19.6%	0.00
Spent time in jail	14.6%	26.7%	9.8%	3.99
Spent time in prison	3.4%	3.3%	−	1.72
Spent time in a residential commitment program	11.2%	13.3%	7.8%	0.64
Was put on nonsecure home detention (including electronic monitoring)	12.4%	16.7%	15.7%	0.01
Was put on probation or community control	24.7%	16.7%	17.6%	0.01
Spent time in a hospital for a physical problem	6.7%	16.7%	17.6%	0.01
Spent time in a hospital for a mental/psychological/emotional problem	2.2%	3.2%	2.9%	0.02
Spent time in a hospital for an alcohol or drug problem	1.1%	−	−	N/A
Spent time in a residential alcohol/other drug program	3.4%	3.3%	−	1.72
Spent time in any other closed facility or program	7.9%	3.3%	2.0%	0.15

Since Baseline Interview, Youth Reported	ESI Youths (n = 89)	FEI Non-Completers (n = 30)	FEI Completers (n = 51)	Chi-Square Value
Was in an outpatient drug treatment or counseling program	3.4%	3.3%	3.9%	0.02
Saw an outpatient counselor, such as a psychologist or psychiatrist	6.7%	6.7%	2.0%	1.17
Spent time in any other outpatient program	1.1%	–	–	N/A

*.10 > p > .05
**p < .05
***p < .01
****p < .001

Appendix E

Percentage of ESI Youths, FEI Noncompleters, and FEI Completers Who Reported Receiving Various Services During the Third Follow-Up Period

Since Baseline Interview, Youth Reported	ESI Youths (n = 44)	FEI Non-Completers (n = 15)	FEI Completers (n = 31)	Chi-Square Value
Was arrested	27.3%	43.3%	25.8%	4.24
Spent time in a juvenile detention center	11.4%	56.3% (n = 16)	9.7%	2.26
Spent time in jail	20.5%	26.7%	12.9%	1.33
Spent time in prison	6.8%	26.7%	3.2%	0.29
Spent time in a residential commitment program	6.8%	6.7%	6.5%	0.00
Was put on nonsecure home detention (including electronic monitoring)	4.5%	6.7%	3.2%	0.50
Was put on probation or community control	27.3%	33.3%	22.6%	0.61
Spent time in a hospital for a physical problem	6.8%	13.3%	9.7%	0.14
Spent time in a hospital for a mental/psychological/ emotional problem	–	–	3.2%	0.50
Spent time in a hospital for an alcohol or drug problem	–	–	–	N/A
Spent time in a residential alcohol/other drug program	–	13.3%	–	2.11
Spent time in any other closed facility or program	9.1%	–	3.2%	0.50

Since Baseline Interview, Youth Reported	ESI Youths (n = 44)	FEI Non-Completers (n = 15)	FEI Completers (n = 31)	Chi-Square Value
Was in an outpatient drug treatment or counseling program	–	–	3.2%	0.50
Saw an outpatient counselor, such as a psychologist or psychiatrist	2.3%	6.7%	2.0%	2.11
Spent time in any other out-patient program	2.3%	–	–	N/A

$*.10 > p > .05$
$**p < .05$
$***p < .01$
$****p < .001$

References

Abelson, R. P. (1985). A variance explanation paradox: When a little is a lot. *Psychological Bulletin* 97: 129-133.

Alexander, J. F. and B. V. Parsons (1982). *Functional family therapy: Principles and procedures*. Carmel, CA: Brooks/Cole.

American Academy of Child and Adolescent Psychiatry (1998). Summary of the practice parameters for the assessment and treatment of children and adolescents with substance use disorders. *Journal of the American Academy of Child and Adolescent Psychiatry* 37: 122-126.

American Correctional Association and Institute for Behavior and Health, Inc. (1991). *Drug testing of juvenile detainees*. Washington, DC: U.S. Department of Justice.

Anglin, M. D., D. Longshore, S. Turner, D. McBride, J. Inciardi, and M. Prendergast (1996). *Studies of the functioning and effectiveness of Treatment Alternatives to Street Crime (TASC) programs: Final report*. Los Angeles: UCLA Drug Abuse Research Center.

Anglin, M. D. and G. Speckart (1988). Narcotics use and crime: A multisample multimethod analysis. *Criminology* 26: 197-233.

Arcia, E., L. Keyes, J. J. Gallagher, and H. Herrick (1993). National portrait of sociodemographic factors associated with underutilization of services: Relevance to early intervention. *Journal of Early Intervention* 17: 283-297.

Armstrong, T. L. and D. M. Altschuler (1998). Recent developments in juvenile aftercare: Assessment, findings, and promising programs. In Roberts, A. R. (Ed.), *Juvenile justice: Policies, programs and services* (pp. 448-472), Second edition. Chicago: Nelson-Hall.

Ashery, R. S. (1992). *Progress and issues in case management*. Rockville, MD: National Institute on Drug Abuse.

Barnes, H. L. and D. H. Olson (1982). *Parent-adolescent communication: Adolescent form, mother form, father form*. Department of Family Social Science. St. Paul: University of Minnesota.

Bateson, G. (1979). *Mind and body*. New York: E. P. Dutton.

Bateson, G., D. Jackson, J. Haley, and J. Weakland (1956). Toward a theory of schizophrenia. *Behavioral Science* 1: 251-264.

Battjes, R. J., L. S. Onken, and P. J. Delany (1999). Drug abuse treatment entry and engagement: Report of a meeting on treatment readiness. *Journal of Clinical Psychology* 55: 643-657.

181

Baumgartner, W. and V. Hill (1996). Hair analysis for organic analyses: Methodology, reliability issues, and field studies. In Kintz, P. (Ed.), *Drug testing in hair* (pp. 223-265). New York: CRC Press.

Bennett, S. and D. Bowers (1976). *An introduction to multivariate techniques for social and behavioral sciences.* New York: John Wiley and Sons.

Bowen, M. (1978). *Family therapy in clinical practice.* New York: Jason Aronson.

Bronfenbrenner, U. (1979). *The ecology of human development: Experiments by nature and design.* Cambridge, MA: Harvard University Press.

Butts, J. A. and A. V. Harrell (1998). *Delinquents or criminals: Policy options for young offenders.* Washington, DC: The Urban Institute.

Catalano, R. F., J. D. Hawkins, E. A. Wells, J. Miller, and D. Brewer (1990-1991). Evaluation of the effectiveness of adolescent drug abuse treatment, assessment of risks for relapse, and promising approaches for relapse prevention. *The International Journal of the Addictions* 25: 1085-1140.

Center for the Study and Prevention of Violence (1999). *Model program selection criteria.* University of Colorado, available: <www.colorado.edu/cspu/blueprints/about/criteria.htm>.

Cervenka, K. A., R. Dembo, and C. H. Brown (1996). A family empowerment intervention for families of juvenile offenders. *Aggression and Violent Behavior* 1: 205-216.

Christensen, A. and N. S. Jacobson (1994). Who (or what) can do psychotherapy: The status and challenge of nonprofessional therapies. *Psychological Science* 5(1): 8-14.

Cocozza, J. J. (1997). Identifying the needs of juveniles with co-occurring disorders. *Corrections Today,* December: 147-149.

Cook, F. (1992). TASC: Case management models linking criminal justice and treatment. In Ashery, R. S. (Ed.), *Progress and issues in case management* (pp. 368-382). Rockville, MD: National Institute on Drug Abuse.

Crimmins, S. M., S. D. Cleary, H. H. Brownstein, B. J. Spunt, and R. M. Warley (2000). Trauma, drugs and violence among juvenile offenders. *Journal of Psychoactive Drugs* 32(1): 43-54.

Demaris, A. (1992). *Logit modeling: Practical applications.* Newbury Park, CA: Sage.

Dembo, R. and R. Brown (1994). The Hillsborough County Juvenile Assessment Center. *Journal of Child and Adolescent Substance Abuse* 3: 25-43.

Dembo, R., K. A. Cervenka, B. Hunter, W. Wang, and J. Schmeidler (1999). Engaging high risk families in community based intervention services. *Aggression and Violence: A Review Journal* 4: 41-58.

Dembo, R., S. Livingston, and J. Schmeidler (2002). Treatment for drug-involved youth in the juvenile justice system. In Leukefeld, C., F. Tims, and D. Farabee (Eds.), *Treatment of drug offenders.* New York: Springer.

Dembo, R., K. Pacheco, J. Schmeidler, G. Ramirez-Garnica, J. Guida, and A. Rahman (1998). A further study of gender differences in service needs among youths entering a juvenile assessment center. *Journal of Child and Adolescent Substance Abuse* 7: 49-77.

Dembo, R., K. Pacheco, J. Schmeidler, L. Fisher, and S. Cooper (1997). Drug use and delinquent behavior among high risk youths. *Journal of Child and Adolescent Substance Abuse* 6: 1-24.

Dembo, R., G. Ramirez-Garnica, M. Rollie, J. Schmeidler, S. Livingston, and A. Hartsfield (2000). Youth recidivism 12 months after a family empowerment intervention: Final report. *Journal of Offender Rehabilitation* 31: 29-65.

Dembo, R., G. Ramirez-Garnica, J. Schmeidler, M. Rollie, S. Livingston, and A. Hartsfield (2001). Long-term impact of a family empowerment intervention on juvenile offenders' recidivism. *Journal of Offender Rehabilitation* 33: 33-57.

Dembo, R., J. Schmeidler, B. Nini-Gough, and D. Manning (1998). Sociodemographic, delinquency-abuse history, and psychosocial functioning differences among juvenile offenders of various ages. *Journal of Child and Adolescent Substance Abuse* 8: 63-78.

Dembo, R., J. Schmeidler, K. Pacheco, S. Cooper, and L. Williams (1997). The relationships between youths' identified substance use, mental health or other problems at a juvenile assessment center and their referrals to needed services. *Journal of Child and Adolescent Substance Abuse* 6: 25-54.

Dembo, R., J. Schmeidler, W. Seeberger, M. Shemwell, L. Klein, M. Rollie, K. Pacheco, S. Livingston, and W. Wothke (2001). Long-term impact of a family empowerment intervention on juvenile offender psychosocial functioning. *Journal of Offender Rehabilitation* 33: 59-109.

Dembo, R. and W. Seeberger (1999). *The need for innovative approaches to meet the substance abuse and mental health service needs of inner-city, African-American youth involved with the juvenile justice system.* Invited paper presented to the U.S. Commission on Civil Rights, Washington, DC, April.

Dembo, R., W. Seeberger, M. Shemwell, J. Schmeidler, L. Klein, M. Rollie, K. Pacheco, A. Hartsfield, and W. Wothke (2000). Psychosocial functioning among juvenile offenders 12 months after family empowerment intervention. *Journal of Offender Rehabilitation* 32: 1-56.

Dembo, R., M. Shemwell, J. Guida, J. Schmeidler, W. Baumgartner, G. Ramirez-Garnica, and W. Seeberger (1999). Comparisons of self-report, urine sample, and hair testing for drug use: A longitudinal study. In Mieczkowski, T. (Ed.), *Drug testing methods: Assessment and evaluation* (pp. 91-107). New York: CRC Press.

Dembo, R., G. Turner, P. Borden, J. Schmeidler, and D. Manning (1995). Screening high risk youths for potential problems: Field application in the use of the Problem Oriented Screening Instrument for Teenagers (POSIT). *Journal of Child and Adolescent Substance Abuse* 3: 69-93.

Dembo, R., G. Turner, J. Schmeidler, C. Chin Sue, P. Borden, and D. Manning (1996). Development and evaluation of a classification of high risk youths entering a juvenile assessment center. *The International Journal of the Addictions* 31: 301-322.

Dembo, R., L. Williams, E. Berry, A. Getreu, M. Washburn, E. D. Wish, and J. Schmeidler (1990). Examination of the relationships among drug use, emotional/psychological problems and crime among youths entering a juvenile detention center. *The International Journal of the Addictions* 25: 1301-1340.

Dembo, R., L. Williams, L. La Voie, E. Berry, A. Getreu, E. Wish, J. Schmeidler, and M. Washburn (1989). Physical abuse, sexual victimization and illicit drug use: Replication of a structural analysis among a new sample of high risk youths. *Violence and Victims* 4: 121-138.

Dembo, R., L. Williams, and J. Schmeidler (1998). A theory of drug use and delinquency among high risk youths. In Roberts, A. R. (Ed.), *Juvenile justice: Policies, programs and services* (pp. 274-311), Second edition. Chicago: Nelson-Hall.

Dembo, R., L. Williams, J. Schmeidler, and C. Christensen (1993). Recidivism in a cohort of juvenile detainees. *The International Journal of the Addictions* 28: 631-657.

Dembo, R., L. Williams, J. Schmeidler, and D. Howitt (1991). *Tough cases: School outreach for at-risk youth*. Office of the Assistant Secretary for Educational Research and Development. Washington, DC: U.S. Department of Education.

Dembo, R., L. Williams, W. Wothke, J. Schmeidler, and C. H. Brown (1992). The role of family factors, physical abuse and sexual victimization experiences in high risk youths' alcohol and other drug use and delinquency: A longitudinal model. *Violence and Victims* 7: 245-266.

Dembo, R., W. Wothke, W. Seeberger, M. Shemwell, K. Pacheco, M. Rollie, J. Schmeidler, L. Klein, A. Hartsfield, and S. Livingston (2000). Testing a model of the influence of family problem factors on high-risk youths' troubled behavior: A three-wave longitudinal study. *Journal of Psychoactive Drugs* 32(1): 55-65.

Dembo, R., W. Wothke, M. Shemwell, K. Pacheco, W. Seeberger, M. Rollie, J. Schmeidler, and S. Livingston (2000). A structural model of the influence of family problems and child abuse factors on serious delinquency among youths processed at a juvenile assessment center. *Journal of Child and Adolescent Substance Abuse* 10: 17-31.

Derogatis, L. D. (1983). *SCL-90-R administration, scoring and procedures manual*. Towson, MD: Clinical Psychometric Research.

Draper, N. R. and H. Smith (1980). *Applied regression analysis,* Second edition. New York: Wiley.

Elliott, D. S., S. S. Ageton, D. Huizinga, B. A. Knowles, and R. J. Canter (1983). *The prevalence and incidence of delinquent behavior: 1976-1980*. Boulder, CO: Behavioral Research Institute.

Espada, F. (1979). The drug abuse industry and the minority communities: Time for change. In Dupont, R. L., A. Goldstein, and J. O'Donnell (Eds.), *Handbook on drug abuse*. Washington, DC: U.S. Government Printing Office.

Faenza, M. M. and C. Siegfried (1998). Responding to the mental health treatment needs of juveniles. *Juvenile Justice Update* 15:3-4.

Finkelhor, D. (1979). *Sexually victimized children*. New York: Free Press.

Fishburne, P. M., H. I. Abelson, and I. Cisin (1980). *National Survey on Drug Abuse: Main Findings—1979*. Rockville, MD: National Institute on Drug Abuse.

Florida Office of Drug Control (2000). *Florida's drug challenge*. Tallahassee: Florida Office of Drug Control.

Grant, B. (2000). Estimates of US children exposed to alcohol abuse and dependence in the family. *American Journal of Public Health* 90(1): 113-115.

Haley, J. (1976). *Problem solving therapy*. San Francisco, CA: Jossey-Bass.

Hanushek, E. A. and J. E. Jackson (1977). *Statistical methods for social scientists*. New York: Academic Press.

Henggeler, S. W. and C. M. Borduin (1990). *Family therapy and beyond: A multisystemic approach to treating the behavior problems of children and adolescents*. Pacific Grove, CA: Brooks/Cole.

Henggeler, S. W., G. B. Melton, L. A. Smith, S. W. Schoenwald, and J. H. Hanley (1993). Family preservation using multi-systemic treatment: Long term follow-up to a clinical trial with serious juvenile offenders. *Journal of Child and Family Studies* 2: 283-293.

Henggeler, S. W., S. K. Schoenwald, S. G. Pickrel, M. J. Brondino, C. M. Borduin, and J. A. Hall (1994). *Treatment manual for family preservation using multi-systemic therapy*. Charleston: Medical University of South Carolina.

Hoffman, L. (1981). *Foundations of family therapy: A conceptual framework for systems change*. New York: Basic Books.

Holm, S. (1979). A single sequentially rejective multiple test procedure. *Scandinavian Journal of Statistics* 6: 65-70.

Hubbard, R. L., M. E. Marsden, J. V. Rachal, H. J. Harwood, E. R. Cavanaugh, and H. M. Ginzburg (1989). *Drug abuse treatment: A national study of effectiveness*. Chapel Hill: The University of North Carolina Press.

Inciardi, J. A., A. E. Pottieger, M. A. Forney, D. D. Chitwood, and D. C. McBride (1991). Prostitution, IV drug use, and sex-for-crack exchanges among serious delinquents: Risks for HIV infection. *Criminology* 29: 221-235.

Jainchill, N., J. Hawke, G. DeLeon, and J. Yagelka (2000). Adolescents in TCs: One-year post-treatment outcomes. *Journal of Psychoactive Drugs* 32: 81-94.

Johnston, L. D., P. M. O'Malley, and J. G. Bachman (1999). *Drug trends in 1999 are mixed*. University of Michigan News and Information Services, Ann Arbor (December). Available: <www.monitoringthefuture.org>, accessed 07/14/00.

Kim, J. and C. E. Mueller (1978). *Factor analysis: Statistical methods and practical issues*. Beverly Hills, CA: Sage.

Klecka, W. R. (1980). *Discriminant analysis*. Beverly Hills, CA: Sage.

Klitzner, M., D. Fisher, K. Stewart, and S. Gilbert (1991). *Report to the Robert Wood Johnson Foundation on strategies for early intervention with children and youth to avoid abuse of addictive substances*. Bethesda, MD: Pacific Institute for Research and Evaluation.

Kumpfer, K. and R. Alvarado (1998). *Effective family strengthening*. Washington, DC: U.S. Department of Justice.

LeBlanc, M. (1990). *Family dynamics, adolescent delinquency and adult criminality*. Paper presented at the Society for Life History Research Conference, Keystone, CO, September.

Leukefeld, C. G. (1991). Opportunities for enhanced drug abuse treatment with criminal justice authority. In Pickens, R. W., C. G. Leukefeld, and C. R. Schuster (Eds.), *Improving drug abuse treatment*. Rockville, MD: National Institute on Drug Abuse.

Lewis, D. O., R. Lovely, C. Yeager, and D. C. Femina (Eds.) (1989). Toward a theory of the genesis of violence: A follow-up study of delinquents. *Journal of the American Academy of Child and Adolescent Psychiatry* 28: 431-436.

Lewis, D. O., S. S. Shanok, J. H. Pincus, and G. H. Glaser (1979). Violent juvenile delinquents, psychiatric, neurological, psychological and abuse factors. *Journal of the American Academy of Child and Adolescent Psychiatry* 18: 307-319.

Lipsey, M. W. and D. B. Wilson (1998). Effective intervention for serious juvenile offenders: A synthesis of research. In Loeber, R. and D. Farrington (Eds.), *Serious and violent juvenile offenders: Risk factors and successful interventions* (pp. 313-344).

McBride, D. C., C. J. VanderWaal, Y. M. Terry, and H. VanBuren (1999). *Breaking the cycle of drug use among juvenile offenders*. Washington, DC: National Institute of Justice.

McGoldrick, M. and R. Gerson (1985). *Genograms in family assessment*. New York: W. W. Norton.

Menard, S. (1995). *Applied logistic regression analysis*. Thousand Oaks, CA: Sage.

Mieczkowski, T., R. Newel, and B. Wraight (1998). Using hair analysis, urinalysis, and self-reports to estimate drug use in a sample of detained juveniles. *Substance Use and Misuse* 33: 1547-1567.

Miller, B. A., W. R. Downs, D. M. Gondoli, and A. Keil (1987). The role of childhood abuse in the development of alcoholism in women. *Violence and Victims* 2:157-172.

Miller, R. G. (1981). *Simultaneous statistical inference,* Second edition. New York: Springer-Verlag.

Minuchin, S. (1974). *Families and family therapy*. Cambridge, MA: Harvard University Press.

Minuchin, S. (1981). *Family therapy techniques*. Cambridge, MA: Harvard University Press.

Minuchin, S. (1984). *Family kaleidoscope*. Cambridge, MA: Harvard University Press.

Mouzakitis, C. W. (1981). Inquiry into the problem of child abuse and juvenile delinquency. In Hunner, R. J. and Y. E. Walker (Eds.), *Exploring the relationship between child abuse and delinquency* (pp. 220-232). Montclair, NJ: Allenheld, Osmun.

National Institute of Justice (1999). *1998 annual report on drug use among adult and juvenile arrestees.* Washington, DC: National Institute of Justice.

National Institute on Drug Abuse (1985). *1985 National Household Survey on Drug Abuse questionnaire.* Rockville, MD: National Institute on Drug Abuse.

Nurco, D. N., M. B. Balter, and T. Kinlock (1994). Vulnerability to narcotic addiction. *Journal of Drug Issues* 24: 293-314.

Office of Juvenile Justice and Delinquency Prevention (2000). *Juvenile Justice Journal: Mental Health Issue,* April.

Office of National Drug Control Policy (1997). *What America's users spend on illegal drugs, 1988-1995.* Washington, DC: Office of National Drug Control Policy.

Olson, D. H. and M. Wilson (1982). *Family satisfaction.* Department of Family Social Science. St. Paul: University of Minnesota.

Personal communication from Florida Department of Juvenile Justice, August 4, 2000.

Pickens, R. W., C. G. Leukefeld, and C. R. Schuster (Eds.) (1991). *Improving drug abuse treatment.* Rockville, MD: National Institute on Drug Abuse.

Rahdert, E. (Ed.) (1991). *The adolescent assessment/referral system.* Rockville, MD: National Institute on Drug Abuse.

Rahdert, E. and D. Czechowicz (Eds.) (1995). *Adolescent drug abuse: Clinical assessment and therapeutic interventions.* Rockville, MD: National Institute on Drug Abuse.

Robbins, M. S. and J. Szapocznik (2000). *Brief strategic family therapy.* Washington, DC: Office of Juvenile Justice and Delinquency Prevention.

Scherer, D. G., M. J. Brondino, S. W. Henggeler, G. B. Melton, and J. H. Hanley (1998). Multisystemic family preservation therapy: Preliminary findings from a study of rural and minority serious adolescent offenders. *Journal of Emotional and Behavioral Disorders* 2:198-206.

Sherman, L., D. Gottfredson, D. McKenzie, J. Eck, P. Reuter, and S. Bushway (1997). *Preventing crime: What works, what doesn't, and what's promising.* Department of Criminology and Criminal Justice. College Park, MD: University of Maryland.

Simpson, D. D., H. K. Wexler, and J. A. Inciardi (Guest Eds.) (1999). Drug treatment outcomes for correctional settings. Special issues of *The Prison Journal,* Part I, 79(3); Part II, 79(4).

Sirles, E. A. (1990). Dropout from intake, diagnostics, and treatment. *Community Mental Health Journal* 26:345-360.

Snyder, H. and M. Sickmund (1995). *Juvenile offenders and victims: A national report.* Washington, DC: Office of Juvenile Justice and Delinquency Prevention.

Snyder, H. and M. Sickmund (1999). *Juvenile offenders and victims: 1999 national report.* Washington, DC: Office of Juvenile Justice and Delinquency Prevention.

Straus, M. A. (1979). Measuring intrafamily conflict and violence: The conflict tactics (CT) scales. *Journal of Marriage and Family* 41:75-88.

Straus, M. A. (1983). Ordinary violence, child abuse, and wife-beating, what do they have in common? In Finkelhor, D., R. J. Gelles, G. T. Hotaling, and M. A. Straus (Eds.), *The dark side of families: Current family violence research.* Beverly Hills, CA: Sage.

Straus, M. A., R. J. Gelles, and S. K. Steinmetz (1980). *Behind closed doors: Violence in the American family.* New York: Doubleday/Anchor.

Straus, M. A., S. L. Hambry, D. Finkelhor, D. W. Moore, and D. Runyan (1998). Identification of child maltreatment with the Parent-Child Conflict Tactic scales: Development and psychometric data for a national sample of American parents. *Child Abuse and Neglect* 22:249-270.

Substance Abuse and Mental Health Services Administration (1997). *National Household Survey on Drug Abuse.* Rockville, MD: Substance Abuse and Mental Health Services Administration.

Substance Abuse and Mental Health Services Administration (2000). *1999 National Household Survey on Drug Abuse.* Rockville, MD: Substance Abuse and Mental Health Services Administration.

Szapocznik, J. and W. M. Kurtines (1989). *Breakthroughs in family therapy with drug-abusing and problem youth.* New York: Springer Publishing Co.

Szapocznik, J. and W. M. Kurtines (1993). Family psychology and cultural diversity: Opportunities for theory, research and application. *American Psychologist* 48: 400-407.

Szapocznik, J., W. M. Kurtines, A. Perez-Vidal, O. E. Hervis, and F. Foote (1990). One person family therapy. In Wells, R. A. and V. A. Gianeti (Eds.), *Handbook of brief psychotherapies.* New York: Plenum.

Teplin, L. A. and J. Swartz (1989). Screening for severe mental disorder in jails: The development of the Referral Decision scale. *Law and Human Behavior* 13:1-18.

Timmons-Mitchell, J., C. Brown, S. C. Schultz, S. E. Webster, L. A. Underwood, and W. Semple (1997). Comparing the mental health needs of female and male incarcerated juvenile delinquents. *Behavioral Sciences and the Law* 15: 195-202.

Tolan, P., K. Ryan, and C. Jaffe (1988). Adolescents' mental health service use and provider, process, and recipient characteristics. *Journal of Clinical Child Psychology* 17: 229-236.

University of Colorado, Center for the Study and Prevention of Violence Model Program Selection Criteria. (1999). Available FTP: 128.138.129.25. File: <www.colorado.edu/cspu/blueprints/about/criteria.htm>.

Weinberg, N. E. Rahdert, J. Colliver, and M. Glantz (1998). Adolescent substance abuse: A review of the past 10 years. *Journal of the American Academy of Child and Adolescent Psychiatry* 37(3): 252-261.

Weisz, J. R., B. Weiss, S. S. Han, D. A. Granger, and B. Norton (1995). Effects of psychotherapy with children and adolescents revisited: A meta-analysis of treatment outcome studies. *Psychological Bulletin* 117: 450-468.

Wexler, H. K., G. Melnick, L. Lowe, and J. Peters (1999). Three-year reincarceration outcomes for Amity in-prison therapeutic community and aftercare in California. *The Prison Journal* 79:321-336.

Widom, C. S. (1989a). Child abuse, neglect, and violent criminal behavior. *Criminology* 27: 251-271.

Widom, C. S. (1989b). The cycle of violence. *Science* 244: 160-166.

Widom, C. S. (1991). Childhood victimization: Risk factor for delinquency. In Colten, M. E. and S. Gore (Eds.), *Adolescent stress: Causes and consequences.* New York: Aldine de Gruyter.

Widom, C. S. (1995). *Victims of childhood sexual abuse—Later criminal consequences.* Washington, DC: U.S. Department of Justice.

Winters, K. C. (1998). *Substance abuse and juvenile offenders.* University of Minnesota. Presentation at Physicians Leadership for National Drug Policy Conference, Washington, DC, November 6.

Winters, K. C. (1999). *Treatment of adolescents with substance use disorders.* Rockville, MD: Center for Substance Abuse Treatment.

Wish, E. D., J. O'Neil, J. A. Crawford, and V. Baldau (1992). Lost opportunity to combat AIDS: Drug users in the criminal justice system. In Mieczkowski, T. (Ed.), *Drugs, crime, and social policy* (pp. 278-298). Boston: Allyn and Bacon.

Index

Abelson, R.P., 107, 136
Agency for Community Treatment
   Services (ACTS), 52

Bonferroni inequality, 154-155
Brief strategic family therapy (BSFT), 10

Case management/referral services, 4-5
Center for the Study and Prevention of
   Violence, 12-13, 97, 110

Elliott, D.S., 74-75
Extended services intervention (ESI), 11

Family. *See also* Intervention programs/
      services
   empowerment, 9, 33
   preservation, 9-12
   structure, 15-18
   therapy, 9-11
   transgenerational perspective, 18-19
Family empowerment intervention
         (FEI). *See also* Field
      consultants; Intervention
      programs/services; Outcome
      analyses; Youth support
      project (YSP)
   activities/implementation manuals,
      20-21, 167-168
   background, 5, 11-12, 15
   clinical policies
      crisis intervention, 43-44
      family/staff safety, 42-43
      working with families, 38-41

Family empowerment intervention
      (FEI) *(continued)*
   cost savings, 12, 159-162, 167
   engagement techniques, 22-23,
      31-32, 38-41, 58, 68, 162
   ensuring integrity of, 44-48
   families served, 31
   goals, 11, 20, 48-49
   intervention strategies, 20-25
   phases, 25-31
   potential improvements in, 162-167
   supervisory personnel, 37-38
   theoretical foundations, 15-20
Field consultants
   guidelines, 26-31
   initial training, 36-37
   in-service training, 44, 47-48
   qualifications, 33-36
   role, 11-12, 32-33
   supervision of, 37-38, 44, 45-47
Finkelhor, D., 69-71
Functional family therapy, 9-10

Genogram, 19, 22

Intervention programs/services. *See
      also* Family empowerment
      intervention (FEI)
   cost effectiveness, 4
   early, 3-4
   entry in/engagement, 8, 19,
      22-23, 31-32, 46-50, 58
   evaluation of, 4, 12-13
   family based, 8-12
   holistic, 2

191

Order a copy of this book with this form or online at:
http://www.haworthpressinc.com/store/product.asp?sku=4652

FAMILY EMPOWERMENT INTERVENTION
An Innovative Service for High-Risk Youths and Their Families

_____ in hardbound at $49.95 (ISBN: 0-7890-1572-2)

_____ in softbound at $29.95 (ISBN: 0-7890-1573-0)

COST OF BOOKS_____

OUTSIDE USA/CANADA/ MEXICO: ADD 20%____

POSTAGE & HANDLING_____
(US: $4.00 for first book & $1.50 for each additional book)
Outside US: $5.00 for first book & $2.00 for each additional book)

SUBTOTAL_____

in Canada: add 7% GST____

STATE TAX____
(NY, OH & MIN residents, please add appropriate local sales tax)

FINAL TOTAL____
(If paying in Canadian funds, convert using the current exchange rate, UNESCO coupons welcome.)

☐ **BILL ME LATER:** ($5 service charge will be added)
(Bill-me option is good on US/Canada/Mexico orders only; not good to jobbers, wholesalers, or subscription agencies.)

☐ Check here if billing address is different from shipping address and attach purchase order and billing address information.

Signature_____

☐ **PAYMENT ENCLOSED: $_____**

☐ **PLEASE CHARGE TO MY CREDIT CARD.**

☐ Visa ☐ MasterCard ☐ AmEx ☐ Discover
☐ Diner's Club ☐ Eurocard ☐ JCB

Account # _____

Exp. Date_____

Signature_____

Prices in US dollars and subject to change without notice.

NAME_____

INSTITUTION_____

ADDRESS_____

CITY_____

STATE/ZIP_____

COUNTRY_____ COUNTY (NY residents only)_____

TEL_____ FAX_____

E-MAIL_____

May we use your e-mail address for confirmations and other types of information? ☐ Yes ☐ No
We appreciate receiving your e-mail address and fax number. Haworth would like to e-mail or fax special discount offers to you, as a preferred customer. **We will never share, rent, or exchange your e-mail address or fax number. We regard such actions as an invasion of your privacy.**

Order From Your Local Bookstore or Directly From
The Haworth Press, Inc.
10 Alice Street, Binghamton, New York 13904-1580 • USA
TELEPHONE: 1-800-HAWORTH (1-800-429-6784) / Outside US/Canada: (607) 722-5857
FAX: 1-800-895-0582 / Outside US/Canada: (607) 722-6362
E-mail: getinfo@haworthpressinc.com
PLEASE PHOTOCOPY THIS FORM FOR YOUR PERSONAL USE.
www.HaworthPress.com

BOF02